Paradoxes

METRO BOOKS
New York

An Imprint of Sterling Publishing
1166 Avenue of the Americas
New York, NY 10036

METRO BOOKS and the distinctive Metro Books logo are registered
trademarks of Sterling Publishing Co., Inc.

ISBN 978-1-4351-6996-8

For information about custom editions, special sales, and premium and
corporate purchases, please contact Sterling Special Sales at 800-805-5489
or specialsales@sterlingpublishing.com

Manufactured in China

2 4 6 8 10 9 7 5 3 1

sterlingpublishing.com

Additional text by Gary Hayden and Michael Picard
Design and illustrations by Matt Windsor

Paradoxes

100 Philosophical Paradoxes
from Achilles to Zeno

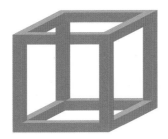

GARETH SOUTHWELL

METRO BOOKS
New York

Contents

What Is a Paradox?

In writing this book about paradoxes, our intention has been to intrigue, baffle, delight, inform, perplex, entertain, and irritate the living hell out of you. Paradoxically, it may even do all of these things.

As you read through these pages, you'll grapple with some of the biggest ideas of all time and become acquainted with some of history's greatest thinkers. Don't worry though, no previous understanding is necessary to enjoy this book; nor do you have to be a math genius to understand the chapters on mathematical and probability paradoxes. The aim is that both those who are more and less familiar with the field of philosophy should be entertained and frustrated in equal measure. If you've never picked up a philosophy book before in your life, it may even inspire you to delve into the works of philosophers such as Plato, Aristotle, Descartes, and David Hume for yourself.

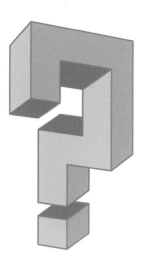

What Makes a Paradox?

In the everyday sense of the word, a paradox is a statement that appears self-contradictory or opposed to common sense but is perhaps true. In this loose sense of the word, we can think of more or less any surprising conclusion, or perhaps anything that contradicts our intuition, as being a form of paradox.

If, however, you're in search of a more philosophical definition, it's hard to beat the British philosopher R. M. Sainsbury's statement that a paradox is "an apparently unacceptable conclusion derived by apparently acceptable reasoning from apparently acceptable premises."

For the purposes of this book, we'll adopt a definition that's somewhere between the two, and say that a paradox is an absurd, contradictory, or counterintuitive conclusion derived from apparently valid reasoning.

Many of the paradoxes in this book have serious implications—serious in the sense of being philosophically, mathematically, or scientifically important—but, we hope, not serious in the sense of being dry or dull.

A number of these paradoxes, such as the Spoof Proofs (see pp. 80–81) or the Missing Dollar Riddle (see pp. 82–83), are not serious at all. In fact, they're not even paradoxes in the strictest sense of the word (though they do fit our rather loose definition, in that their absurd conclusions are derived from apparently valid reasoning). Purists may be scandalized to find them here—but they're too much fun to leave out.

So, what else might you find within these pages? Well, one example is the Italian scientist Galileo's very simple and succinct proof that there are fewer square numbers (1, 4, 9, 16, 25, and so on) than there are natural numbers (1, 2, 3, 4, 5, and so on). At the same time, he gave an almost identical proof that there are just as many squares as naturals.

Check out Galileo's Paradox (see pp. 88–89) and you'll see that his reasoning can't be faulted in either case. So, Galileo demonstrated that the natural numbers outnumber the squares; and he also demonstrated that they don't. That's what you call a paradox.

Here's another example: In the fifth century BCE, Zeno of Elea came up with a very elegant proof that the swiftest athlete can never overtake the slowest-moving tortoise (see pp. 128–129). Of course, we know that this is absurd. Athletes clearly can overtake tortoises. Yet spotting the flaw in Zeno's argument is notoriously difficult—so much so that people are still arguing about it two-and-a-half thousand years later.

In short, the paradoxes you'll encounter are many and varied, from game-show puzzles that have a surprising solution to major discoveries that have changed the world.

How to Read This Book

This is not a book to be read passively. The more you engage with the text the more fun you will have, and the more easily understood the problems become. You'll often be asked to stop and think things through; but be careful, some of these paradoxes will lodge themselves in your mind and worry away at you. Some may even keep you awake at night.

There are also thought experiments and challenges to stretch your mind—but don't keep them to yourself, why not try them out on your family and friends and keep them from sleeping as well?

Like a good puzzle, we hope this book will infuriate and delight you in equal measure. So go ahead, expand your mind, strain your brain, and, above all, have fun!

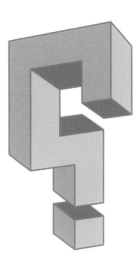

Before we dive into our first set of paradoxes, let's stop and take a look at what lies ahead. This book can be read from cover to cover, but it does not have to be. Obviously, there are advantages to reading through the book in such a methodical way, but you can also dip into and out of the pages or chapters as you wish.

Many of the paradoxes are self-contained to be read in a few minutes, but provide enough intellectual stimulation to last a lifetime.

So, before you get going, here is a brief guide to what lies within each of the chapters.

Chapter 1

Knowing and Believing launches our voyage into the paradoxical by challenging what we know to be true, or at least what we think we know.

Chapter 2

Vagueness and Identity plumbs the gray areas of language and ideas, and introduces some of the classic paradoxes of philosophy that concern them.

Chapter 3

Logic and Truth poses some fascinating practical puzzles, before moving on to more abstract, but equally intriguing problems of reference and membership.

Chapter 4

Mathematical Paradoxes starts small with a few perplexing puzzles and their counterintuitive solutions, before working up to the mind-blowing world of infinity.

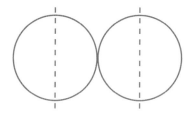

Chapter 5

Probability Paradoxes shows just how vulnerable our grasp of practical math can be; it swiftly leads via a popular game show to Blaise Pascal's rationale for believing in God.

Chapter 6

Space and Time explores the strange things that happen when you start dividing time, and also looks at the weird problems posed by the possibility of time travel.

Chapter 7

Impossibilities are those things that simply can't exist. Nevertheless, this chapter takes a look at several of them, from popular optical illusions to what God is or isn't capable of.

Chapter 8

Deciding and Acting are inextricably linked to our daily lives, but how we should decide, and indeed how we should act, isn't always as obvious as it might at first seem.

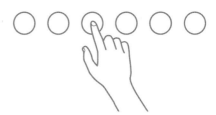

Throughout the chapters you'll find mini-features on key philosophers and scientists who have worked in the fields discussed. Then, at the end of the book there's a handy index of notable philosophers, as well as a selected list of references.

Chapter 1

Knowing and Believing

Seeming to know can be so much like knowing that it is hard to know in the end which is which, and as a result all knowing appears to be mere seeming to know. Do not ask *what we know*; ask rather *what it is to know. What does it mean to know? What is knowledge?* We contemplate birds, butterflies, lotteries, emeralds, memories, placebos, and dreams not to learn more about these bits of reality, but to expose the paradoxes that patrol the perimeter of epistemology.

The Paradox of Ignorance

How do we know that we know what we think we know? Rather than answer this question, the Greek philosopher Socrates, mentor to Plato, turned the question on its head: rather than profess our certainty on any subject, isn't it wiser to acknowledge the boundaries of our own ignorance? Or, as he famously put it, "I do not claim to know what I do not know."

According to Plato (who relates the story in the *Apology*), Socrates's follower Chaerephon once asked the oracle of Delphi who was the wisest of men, to which she replied that Socrates was. On hearing this information, Socrates became puzzled, until he realized that the oracle must mean that he was only wise because, unlike others who mistakenly claimed knowledge they did not really possess, only Socrates knew that he knew nothing.

Socratic Method

This attitude has formed the basis of what has become known as the *Socratic method*, which is—depending on how you use it—either a cunning debating technique or a sincere attempt to arrive at truth. So, rather than build up and defend a philosophical theory, you simply seek out those who claim they know something, and then question why they think they know it. Either you will prove the other person an idiot, or both of you will arrive at a deeper appreciation of the issue. And, to the great annoyance of many, this is what Socrates famously did, scouring the Athenian populace for those who might provide him with that knowledge he lacked.

Can We Really Know We Know Nothing?

It is in fact debatable whether the actual Socrates did indeed profess such radical ignorance, for not only is our chief source for his life and opinions the writing of his most famous pupil (Plato), but those writings themselves often portray Socrates as laying claim to all sorts of knowledge (leaving us unsure as to what is Socrates and what is Plato . . .). But even if he did make such a claim, can we really know that we know nothing? Isn't knowledge of our own ignorance *itself* a form of knowledge? Thus, there seems to be a paradox: to know that I know nothing I must at least know something (that I know nothing), and therefore I cannot be said to know nothing.

To be fair to Socrates (or at least, Plato's version of him), he does not strictly claim to know nothing, but only that he does not lay claim to that which he does not know. But is this any less paradoxical? As the Austrian philosopher Ludwig Wittgenstein put it, "In order to be able to set a limit to thought, we should have to find both sides of the limit thinkable." Wittgenstein is talking about language here, but the principle would also seem to apply to knowledge: in order to know that I know nothing, it would seem that I have to have some basis by which I divide things up into those things I know, and those I don't. And in order to do that, it seems logical that I have to state *why* I know the things I do—which takes us right back to the initial problem of *how* I know what I claim to know. So, depending on how you interpret it, either Socrates's claim is paradoxical (to know that you know nothing is at least to know something), or else it requires knowledge that has troubled philosophers before and since (on what basis we can claim that we truly know something). Either way, a claim of ignorance would seem to be no less paradoxical than a claim to knowledge.

THE ORACLE AT DELPHI

The Pythia was the high priestess of the Temple of Apollo in Delphi in ancient Greece, one of the most famous oracles in the classical world. Her sanctuary on the slopes of Mount Parnassus was a common destination for kings and emperors before they undertook momentous decisions.

On one such occasion, King Croesus of Lydia asked her advice as to whether he should go to war against the Persian Empire, receiving the reply that doing so would ruin a great empire. Taking this as a sign to proceed, he attacked Persia, only to find out too late that, ironically, the empire that was to be ruined was in fact his own.

Perhaps to avoid the displeasure of such powerful patrons, the oracle's pronouncements often took such an ambiguous form. In this case, we can see that she would have been right no matter what the result.

Meno's Paradox

Related to the problem of Socratic ignorance is what has come to be known as Meno's Paradox. In the Platonic dialogue the *Meno*, Socrates admits that although a problem or contradiction sometimes reveals when an idea is wrong, how do we know when we're right? Meno's response is to doubt the possibility of the search for knowledge itself: either, he says, we know what we're looking for, in which case what's the point in looking for something we already know; or else we don't know, in which case we'll never find it anyway. And so, the whole search for knowledge is paradoxical. Is Meno right?

Let's say I don't know the capital of Moldova, so I do a web search and find out that it's Chişinău. Now, Meno's argument implies that to claim this new information as knowledge, either I already knew that it was Chişinău, or I cannot now be sure that it is in fact Chişinău, because I didn't previously know it. It's possible, of course, that I'm wrong—I've misread something, used an unreliable source or out-of-date information, but assuming none of these to be true, it would seem Meno is asking the impossible: in order to possess knowledge, we must already have it.

Sophistry

Most philosophers now consider Meno's argument a form of sophistry or logical trick. To illustrate this, let's take a different example. You're doing a jigsaw, and to your great consternation the final piece is missing. But it's one of those fiendish jigsaws that doesn't show the final picture on the box. Now, as you look for it—under the couch, inside the cat's bed, among other jigsaws—you have a vague idea of what the piece should look like. It's in the middle of a patch of bushes that have pink flowers, so it should be green and pink, with a certain shape. You don't know exactly what the piece looks like, but you have a rough idea, and you're fairly confident you'll know it when you see it.

MENO'S SLAVE

Plato's proposed solution to Meno's paradox involves the attempt to show that knowledge is somehow innate, or present from birth.

To illustrate this, he questions a young boy, a slave in Meno's house, as to Pythagoras's famous theorem concerning the nature of right-angled triangles. The boy has no mathematical education, and yet—via Socrates's carefully formulated questions—he is led to demonstrate an apparently intuitive knowledge of this concept.

Thus, Plato concludes, education is not so much about putting knowledge in, as drawing knowledge out.

Is he right? If you track down Plato's original text, you will see that Socrates's questions are more than a little leading (as a lawyer might point out), and we certainly can't say that the boy arrives at this "knowledge" of his own accord. However, we might also concede Plato's point: to learn something, we first need a framework for it to fit into—perhaps, then, it's *this* that's innate.

Meno's Trick

And here's Meno's trick: knowing what would fit is different to knowing the detail on the missing piece. And the same is true of knowledge in general. In searching for something we don't know, we often presume the missing information will fit with other things we know. An astrophysicist observes an irregular orbit in a distant planet, but doesn't know why; however, based on their understanding of mass and gravity, while they don't know exactly what's causing the irregularity, they have candidates (a black hole, another previously undiscovered planet, or whatever).

So, while Meno's puzzle isn't really a paradox, it reveals something interesting about knowledge: to know something, we must know the type of thing to look for. This is why Plato did not simply dismiss Meno's argument as fallacious, but admitted that there was some truth behind it, for there's a sense in which all our knowledge is recollection. Now, Plato frames this in terms of the soul's ability to "remember" things based on the forms of knowledge divinely imprinted upon it, and which gives us a sort of head start in life.

What Is Possible to Know?

Kant makes a similar point in less mystical terms, arguing that what we are able to know is shaped in advance by the nature of human reason and perception. In other words, we can only know what it is possible for us to know, given the way our human faculties work, the ideas we are fitted to grasp. Of course, this means that there are things that will be forever beyond our comprehension—not that we can actually know that, of course.

The Cartesian Circle

Having arrived at the *cogito*—that he, as a thinking thing, can't doubt his own existence—Descartes believed he saw a way to provide a secure basis for knowledge in general (*foundationalism*). However, this attempt famously involved what seems to be a paradox—something that's since become known as *the Cartesian Circle*.

To arrive at the cogito, Descartes entertained three increasingly radical scenarios or waves of doubt: his senses can never be trusted; there's no way of telling dream from reality; and some all-powerful, malign entity could potentially deceive him about everything. In relation to this last point, he finally realized that even such a being couldn't convince him he didn't exist. But why? Here's where things begin to unravel.

Logic Versus Perception

Descartes argued that the certainty of the cogito lay in its being clearly and distinctly true. Some things we experience are fuzzy and indistinct: a pain in your side may give you no clear idea as to what's causing it; a fleeting impression can leave you unsure whether a distant object is a bird or a plane—such reasons convinced Descartes to reject the evidence of the senses in the first place. In contrast, ideas such as the cogito and certain principles of mathematics or truths of logic, are radically different. The fact that 2 + 2 = 4 doesn't change from moment to moment, nor is its truth subjective, varying from person to person. As long as we stick with ideas that have this stamp of approval, then we should be fine. But how do we know we can trust this stamp of approval?

That hypothetical demon is, remember, all powerful. What makes clear and distinct ideas themselves trustworthy? Descartes's answer is, unfortunately, God, who isn't deceitful, and has furnished humans with the capacity to clearly and distinctly perceive that certain ideas are true. I say "unfortunately" here because now Descartes must prove that God exists. And how does he do that?

Does God Exist?

There are a few arguments for the existence of God in Descartes's *Meditations*. For instance, there's the Trademark Argument: I seem to have the idea of an infinite being; since I am myself a finite being, I can't have created that idea myself, and it doesn't seem to have come from anywhere else; therefore, God Himself must have placed it in my mind from birth—a sort of trademark or signature left by the craftsman. Or, there's the Ontological Argument: since God is, by traditional definition, a perfect being, wouldn't it be an imperfection in Him not to exist? Therefore, He must.

It's not important here whether you find such arguments convincing—and philosophers have debated their pros and cons for centuries—but rather what's important is the role that they play in

Descartes's scheme to secure knowledge in general. And here's the problem: even if his arguments for the existence of God are logically flawless, how can he trust them? Because, as with mathematics or the cogito, they are clear and distinctly true. And what guarantees that clear and distinct ideas are true? That God exists. And what guarantees God's existence? The logical arguments that clearly and distinctly demonstrates that He exists . . . It's a vicious circle, a paradox.

But lest you think this problem is confined to theists, ponder this: how can you be sure that $2 + 2 = 4$? If you argue that it's logically irrefutable, or contradictory to deny, what guarantees that such standards are themselves trustworthy? It would seem that any attempt to provide a reason for why particular fundamental truths are certain is itself open to question. And such is the problem of foundationalism.

FOUNDATIONALISM

Descartes argues that in order to know something, we must base it ultimately on something that is itself beyond doubt. This approach—known as foundationalism—therefore seeks to identify absolutely certain "foundations" for our beliefs.

However, as we've seen, not only is such an approach problematic, but we might also question whether it's necessary. An alternative approach is coherentism, where beliefs are judged on whether they fit with other things we have good reason to believe. And so, if

Descartes's approach may be visualized as a sort of upside-down pyramid, with the core beliefs sitting at the bottom, coherentism may be seen as a jigsaw, where we must decide whether the new pieces improve the overall "picture."

However, this approach too comes with its own problems: for centuries, astronomers and theologians rejected evidence that contradicted geocentrism (the idea that the Earth was at the center of the universe) simply because it didn't "fit."

Gettier Problems

What is knowledge? Plato's definition, first proposed in his *Theaetetus*, was for a long time accepted by subsequent philosophers: knowledge is a form of justified true belief. We know something if and only if our opinion is true, and we have strong evidence to support it. At first, this seems to be a sensible definition. It rules out lucky guesses, or strongly supported but ultimately false beliefs. Of course, there are still possible problems with aspects of the theory; as we will see in relation to the Lottery paradox, there is a question as to how much supporting evidence may be considered enough. There's also the related question of whether someone should be allowed to say they "know" things when absolute certainty is arguably beyond our reach—it seems harsh to simply ban use of the verb "to know"! But for many years, Plato's tripartite definition of knowledge has largely been accepted.

The turning point came in a 1963 article by Edmund Gettier, which proposed that there were conceivable situations in which Plato's criteria might be met, but yet in which we would still not wish to grant that there was knowledge. One of the examples Gettier gives concerns two men, Smith and Jones, who apply for the same job. Now, Smith has good reasons to believe two things: (1) Jones will get the job, and (2) Jones has ten coins in his pocket. (We don't really need to worry as to why or how Smith knows these particular things—perhaps he's had a reliable tip-off, perhaps he's seen Jones counting his cash while they wait to be interviewed—we just need to assume that they're strong reasons.) Now, because he is sure of both these things, he forms the belief that (3) "the man who gets the job will have ten coins in his pocket." However, as it turns out, it is Smith himself who gets the job, and—what a coincidence!—he himself has ten coins in his pocket! Now, while Smith would seem to be right in his belief, but for the wrong reasons, that doesn't actually matter, because he would seem to meet all Plato's criteria: he believes (3), he has strong reasons to believe (3) is true, and (3) actually is true. But this isn't right, surely? And this is Gettier's point: most people would agree that Smith's belief doesn't constitute knowledge, and yet Plato's widely accepted definition does not seem to be able to say why.

Justifying a True Belief

Since Gettier's article, philosophers have therefore lined up to plug the gap Gettier highlighted. For instance, Alvin Goldman proposed that a belief is only justified if it has been caused in the appropriate way: Smith's belief that the successful candidate would have ten coins in his pocket was caused by noting that this was true of Jones (not realizing it was also true of himself), and so there was no direct causal connection between his evidence

DEFINING KNOWLEDGE

Defining knowledge remains problematic —Plato himself found problems with his own proposed tripartite definition. An alternative approach was proposed by Austrian philosopher Ludwig Wittgenstein, who argued that such problems of definition arise from failure to appreciate that language isn't a rigorously logical affair, and that concepts themselves are embedded in social behavior and practice.

Consider defining the word "game": not all games involve competition, so making that an essential criterion would exclude things like hopscotch or clapping games; conversely, defined too broadly, we might include things that definitely aren't games—such as warfare. This is because "game" does not describe a single or fixed set of criteria, but rather a network of meanings that are related, much like the members of a family.

For Wittgenstein, then, rather than defining knowledge, we should look instead to understand the concept in relation to the limits and conventions of language.

and his belief. Alternatively, Keith Lehrer and Thomas Paxson proposed that a true belief is justified as long as there is no other truth that, had someone known it, would have caused them to revise their belief (if Smith had known that Jones would not get the job, he would have revised his belief about the number of coins in the successful candidate's pocket).

Of course, none of this is itself strictly paradoxical; it merely reveals that Plato's criteria (and subsequent attempts to refine them) are inadequate. The bigger problem, however, is that, as the controversy trundles on, we seem to be no nearer an acceptable solution. Does this mean that—paradoxically—a clear definition of knowledge is itself something that cannot be known?

Two Paradoxes Concerning Belief

During a lecture, the English philosopher G. E. Moore (1873–1958) once remarked on the absurdity of saying something like, "It's raining outside, but I don't believe that it is." When Ludwig Wittgenstein (1889–1951) heard about this he was very much struck by the paradoxical nature of the statement. In fact, he considered it Moore's most important philosophical discovery, and labeled it "Moore's Paradox."

At first sight, it's difficult to see what all the fuss is about. Certainly, the statement is absurd. But, then again, many statements are absurd. What's so special about this one?

Well, in the first place, it's clear that both parts of Moore's statement can be true simultaneously. It is perfectly possible that (1) It's raining outside, and (2) I don't believe that it's raining outside. There's no absurdity there. Furthermore, I can assert either proposition individually, without absurdity. Not only that, but it's perfectly acceptable to assert both propositions simultaneously with reference to a third party: "It's raining outside, but she doesn't believe that it is." And, to cap it all, I can consistently make both statements with reference to myself provided I use the past tense: "It was raining outside, but I didn't believe it was."

The paradox, then, is that although the two propositions are not at all opposed to one another, I cannot consistently assert them both. But how can it be contradictory to say something which, in itself, is not contradictory?

Given all that has been said, why can't I say, "It's raining outside, but I don't believe that it is"? Mull this over before reading on.

A Possible Resolution

There is no definitive resolution to Moore's Paradox. The most popular approach, which Moore himself took, hinges on the notion that assertion implies belief. In other words, my assertion that it's raining carries with it the implication that I believe that it's raining. If so, then the statement, "It's raining outside, but I don't believe that it is," turns out to be contradictory after all. Effectively it says, "I believe that it is raining, but I don't believe that it is."

The Placebo Paradox

As Moore's Paradox demonstrates, beliefs are tricky things. Further evidence of their weirdness comes from the Placebo Paradox, which was invented by Peter Cave, and goes something like this:

A placebo in itself has no pharmaceutical properties: it works only because I believe it will. So it is not the placebo, but rather my belief in it, that cures me. What happens, then, if I know that I'm taking a placebo? In that case, the placebo will be ineffective. The placebo cures me only because I believe it will, but I cannot believe that it will cure me only because I believe it will.

There are shades of Moore's Paradox here. I can believe that a placebo will cure you only because you believe it will. For that matter I can even believe that a placebo did cure me only because I believed it would. However, I cannot believe that a placebo will cure me only because I believe it will.

THE WILL TO BELIEVE

From childhood until my late twenties I [Gary Hayden] attended a church whose members believed that the "prayer of faith" could heal the sick. Sadly, we never got to see any healings worth a damn.

Many times, this dearth of miracles was blamed on our unbelief. The Bible says: "[Jesus] did not do many miracles there because of their unbelief," (Matt. 13:58). So that told us, I guess. We were therefore encouraged to lay aside our unbelief; and most of us tried very hard to do precisely that. But it was a catch-22 situation. God wouldn't perform any miracles until we believed; and we couldn't believe until God performed some miracles.

But perhaps I'm being cynical. Maybe it's possible to acquire certain beliefs by a mere act of will. The mathematician, scientist, and philosopher Blaise Pascal certainly thought so. (See pp. 120–121.)

Profile

René Descartes

"Some years ago I noticed how many false things I had accepted as true in my childhood, and how doubtful were the things that I subsequently built on them…"
—Descartes, Meditation I

The French philosopher René Descartes (1596–1650) lived during a period of great intellectual upheaval. The educational institutions of his time were controlled by the Church and delivered a curriculum based firmly upon the authority of ancient texts, such as the Bible and the works of Aristotle.

At the same time, the modern scientific conception of knowledge, with its emphasis on free enquiry and firsthand research, was beginning to assert itself. As a result, many of the old "certainties"—for example, that the sun orbits the earth—were being demolished.

Descartes was a first-rate philosopher, mathematician, and scientist. As such, he became acutely aware of the shortcomings of his early education, which had led him to accept as being true much that had subsequently been proved false. He didn't want to make the same kind of error again. So he set himself the task of placing the new scientific method on a secure footing. He saw himself as a master builder, tearing down the old, crumbling edifice of knowledge, and rebuilding it anew upon rock-solid foundations.

The Method of Doubt

To achieve his aim, Descartes used what has become known as the Method of Doubt. This involved him systematically rejecting any of his old beliefs that he could find the slightest reason to doubt. This, he hoped, would leave him with indubitable knowledge, which could serve as a bedrock for the new sciences.

The Method of Doubt progressed in three stages, each more sweeping than the last.

Stage 1: Unreliable Senses

"Everything that I accepted as being most true up to now I acquired … through the senses. However, I have occasionally found that they deceive me."

The senses sometimes deceive us. For example: the moon appears to be bigger when it is closer to the horizon, hot weather can make a dry road look wet, a circular coin looks oval when viewed at certain angles, and so on. Therefore we have to be cautious about accepting the evidence of our senses.

Even so, surely some observations are reliable. For example, can you really doubt that you are now reading these very words?

Stage 2: Dream Hypothesis

"Very well. But am I not a man who is used to sleeping at night and having all the same experiences while asleep?"

On second thought, perhaps your belief that you are here, reading this book, is mistaken. After all, you could be dreaming.

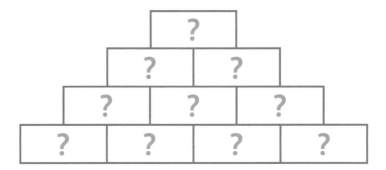

Our dream-experiences often feel perfectly real to us while we are having them. So how can you be absolutely certain that you're not asleep right now—dreaming about reading this book?

There is no foolproof way of distinguishing between being awake and being asleep. Therefore you can't be completely sure that your present experiences are veridical.

But, even if you are dreaming, you can be sure that your dreams are based on something. True, you may not be holding this book in your hand right now. But surely there must be such things as hands and books. Otherwise how would you dream about them?

Stage 3: The Evil Genius

"Therefore, I will suppose that … some evil mind, who is all powerful and cunning, has devoted all [his] energies to deceiving me."

But, then again, perhaps everything is a delusion. Perhaps some demon or "evil genius" is manipulating your mind, causing you to believe all kinds of things that have no basis in reality.

Perhaps there are no such things as hands and books—or trees, or sunsets, or colors, or shapes. Perhaps the evil genius has you so bamboozled that even things you feel absolutely certain of, like the fact that one plus one equals two, are mere delusions.

But if I allow that possibility, how can I be sure of anything? Surely nothing can withstand such all-consuming doubt?

I Think, Therefore …

It is worth emphasizing that Descartes wasn't seriously suggesting that an evil genius might be deceiving him. He was using hyperbolic doubt as a tool to conduct a thought experiment in order to see if any knowledge is immune to doubt.

Unbelievably, he found something. The one thing he couldn't doubt was his own existence, because the very act of thinking, doubting, or even being deceived presupposes it.

This simple but beautiful insight prompted Descartes to pen philosophy's most celebrated catchphrase: "I think, therefore I am."

Having at last reached a secure foundation, Descartes went on to rebuild the edifice of knowledge. How he achieved this (at least to his own satisfaction) is laid out in his beautifully written *Meditations on First Philosophy*.

Butterfly Dreams

"Once upon a time, I, Chuang Tzu, dreamed I was a butterfly, fluttering hither and thither, to all intents and purposes a butterfly. I was conscious only of following my fancies as a butterfly, and was unconscious of my individuality as a man. Suddenly I awoke, and there I lay, myself again. Now I do not know whether I was then a man dreaming I was a butterfly, or whether I am now a butterfly dreaming I am a man."

This delicious paradox comes from the Chinese philosopher Chuang Tzu. His experiences support the notion that he is a man who dreamed of being a butterfly; but equally they support the notion that he is a butterfly who dreams of being a man. The former option strikes us as by far the more feasible. But why?

Most people would respond that the butterfly episode occurs merely as a brief interlude amid a whole lifetime of human experiences. But how do we know that dreams are characterized by brevity?

Life Is But a Dream

Chuang Tzu mused over his butterfly dream in about the fourth century BCE. At much the same time, over in Athens, Plato (428–348 BCE) wrestled with essentially the same problem. In Plato's dialogue *Theaetetus*, the character Socrates declares:

"You see, then, it is not difficult to find matter for dispute, when it is disputed even whether this is real life or a dream. Indeed, we may say that, as our periods of sleeping and waking are of equal length, and as in each period the soul contends that the beliefs of the moment are preeminently true, the result is that for half our lives we assert the reality of the one

set of objects, and for half that of the other set. And we make our assertions with equal conviction in both cases."

Real and Unreal

What if things didn't have to be either real or unreal, but could be both? The possibility of a similarly surreal duality was touched upon by the Austrian physicist Erwin Schrödinger in a thought experiment known as Schrödinger's Cat.

In his famous paradox, Schrödinger imagines a cat placed inside a closed box where a random subatomic occurrence, such as a radioactive decay, releases a poisonous gas. According to the "Copenhagen Interpretation" of quantum mechanics, at a tiny scale a particle exists not in one state, but in a combination of all possible states—the state only becomes definite when observed. Schrödinger extrapolates this to the bizarre situation in which, until the box is opened, the cat is simultaneously dead and alive.

This is sometimes viewed as a reductio ad absurdum argument (see pp. 84–85) against the Copenhagen Interpretation. More often, though, it is seen as illustrating the kind of weirdness that goes on at the quantum level.

STOP AND THINK

Perhaps in the argument he puts forward Socrates is being a tiny bit mischievous, but he raises some very interesting questions.

- How can we be sure that what we call "reality" is not a dream, and that what we call "dreams" are not reality?

- Could it be that the whole of life is a dream, and that what we call "dreams" are really dreams-within-a-dream?

On a separate note, in the first of his *Meditations*, the French philosopher René Descartes (see pp. 22–23) wrote: "I see so clearly that I can never distinguish, by reliable signs, being awake from being asleep." Did he miss something? Do you have any means of knowing, with absolute certainty, whether you are awake or asleep right now?

THE FAB FOUR

Back in the late 1970s, when I was in my early teens, I became a Beatles fan. By then, the Fab Four had been disbanded for almost a decade. So, although I liked their music, I knew very little about them as individuals.

One night, I dreamed I was watching a T.V. documentary, which informed me that John, Paul, George, and Ringo, in addition to being pop stars, had all played professional soccer for Liverpool F.C. (In my mind's eye, I can still see the documentary footage of them running around the field at the Anfield stadium.)

The funny thing is that for weeks afterward I wasn't sure whether I had dreamed it or not. Sure, it seemed extremely unlikely that the Beatles had all been top soccer players. But, then again, the dream—if dream it was—was so very, very vivid.

I've since learned that the Beatles never did play professional soccer. So now I know I was dreaming.

Unless, of course, I've merely dreamed that I've since learned that they never played soccer!

The Lottery

Imagine a fair lottery with a million tickets. It's exceedingly unlikely that a given ticket will win; therefore we are justified in believing it will lose. But the same reasoning applies to every ticket. So we are justified in believing that every ticket will lose, even though we know that one of them will win.

Our first thought on encountering the lottery paradox might be to dismiss it with a shrug of the shoulders. It sounds suspiciously like mere verbal trickery. The leap from "it is exceedingly unlikely that a given ticket will win" to "we are justified in believing that it will lose" seems tenuous, to say the least.

But, like many philosophical conundrums, this one repays closer inspection. So let's dig a little deeper …

Justified Belief

How much certainty is required in order for a belief to be justified? Or, putting it another way, how great a possibility of error can a justified belief withstand? For example, as I write this, I am sitting in a coffee shop in Ho Chi Minh City, Vietnam drinking a diet cola. I know that it's a diet cola because that's what I ordered, and because it came to me in a diet cola can.

Surely, no one would deny that I'm justified in believing that I'm drinking diet cola. Nonetheless, I could be mistaken. The people at the cola factory may have filled my can with full-sugar cola by mistake. Or maybe this coffee shop serves fake, full-sugar cola in authentic-looking diet cola cans. It's even possible that I'm only dreaming I'm drinking diet cola (see pp. 23–25).

All of these alternatives seem pretty unlikely, so let's estimate the odds that I'm mistaken at, say, a million-to-one. In that case, my belief that I'm drinking diet cola is justified, even though there's a million-to-one chance I'm wrong.

Back to the Lottery…

So, there's a million-to-one chance that I'm not drinking diet cola, just as there's a million-to-one chance that any individual lottery ticket will win. Nonetheless,

Lottery
05 / 12 / 19 / 27 / 38

03   07

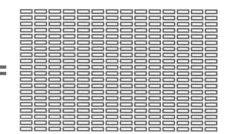

my belief that I'm drinking diet cola is justified. Therefore my belief that the lottery ticket will lose must be justified too.

Now, perhaps, we can return to the Lottery Paradox with renewed respect. It seems that we are, after all, justified in believing that each and every individual lottery ticket will lose, even though we know that one of them must win. Thus we hold inconsistent, but apparently justified, beliefs.

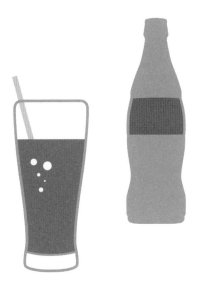

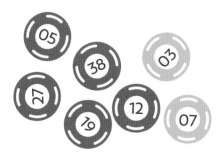

Think It Through

Here are two possible responses to the lottery paradox. Which of them appeals to you most?

First, we can deny that we know a given ticket will lose. Contrary to what the paradox assumes, there is no justification for believing that a given ticket will lose. And, in fact, no one does believe it. Quite the reverse. Everyone knows that all lottery tickets stand a chance, however small, of winning. Otherwise people wouldn't buy them.

This neatly disposes of the paradox, but raises a question. Why is it that I can't claim to know that a given ticket will lose, whereas I can claim to know that I'm currently drinking diet cola? Isn't there a similar chance of error in both cases?

Alternatively, we can tighten up the criteria for knowledge. The lottery paradox relies upon the assumption that a belief can be justified even when there is a possibility of error. So to avoid the paradox, we simply tighten up the rules and say that a belief can only be justified (we can only know something) if there is no possibility of error.

This avoids the paradox—but at a price. It means that there is little, if anything, that we can truly know. This idea is related to Descartes's thoughts outlined on pp. 22–23.

Profile

David Hume

The Scottish philosopher David Hume (1711–1776) is widely regarded as one of the all-time greats. He was intensely interested in what philosophers call epistemological questions—that is, questions about what we can know, and how we can know it.

His works, including *A Treatise of Human Nature* and the posthumously published *Dialogues Concerning Natural Religion*, are enormously influential and a delight to read.

Relations of Ideas and Matters of Fact

"All the objects of human reason or enquiry may naturally be divided into two kinds, to wit, Relations of Ideas, and Matters of fact," (Hume, *An Enquiry Concerning Human Understanding*).

According to Hume, there are two—and only two—valid fields of human investigation: relations of ideas, and matters of fact. Arithmetic, geometry, algebra, and the like are concerned with relations of ideas. Arithmetical statements, such as "Two plus three equals five," can be known and understood by a process of pure thought, since they merely express relationships between various numbers. Similarly, geometrical propositions like "The internal angles of a triangle add up to 180°" merely express relationships between concepts such as "angle," "triangle," and so on. Such truths can be known with

absolute certainty. Indeed, they cannot be denied without contradiction. It is not merely wrong to deny that "Two plus three is equal to five," it is demonstrably absurd.

Matters of fact, on the other hand, are not merely statements about ideas; they are statements about the world. For example, "The sun is bigger than the moon," "Dropped stones fall to the ground," and "This ink is black." The only way to establish the truth or falsity of matters of fact is to investigate how things are out there in the world. No amount of abstract philosophical speculation could ever establish that "This ink is black."

Unlike relations of ideas, which can be demonstrably proven, matters of empirical fact cannot be known with absolute certainty. There is always the possibility, however slight, that we may be mistaken (see pp. 26–27).

Hume's Fork

To recap, there are two—and only two—valid fields of human investigation: relations of ideas and matters of fact. This leads to an important principle, often referred to as Hume's Fork.

When presented with any putative item of knowledge we can ask ourselves two questions: "Is it derived from relations of ideas?" and "Is it a matter of empirical fact?" If the answer to both questions is no, then that item of so-called knowledge is pure baloney—however clever-sounding it may be.

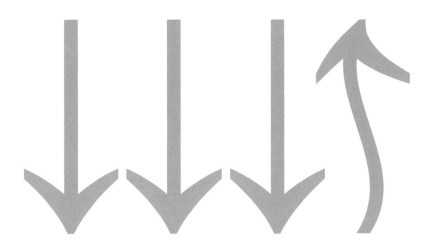

This simple but powerful insight led Hume to reject all abstract philosophical speculation concerning such matters as the nature of God and the existence of the soul:

"If we take in our hand any volume; of divinity or school metaphysics, for instance; let us ask, Does it contain any abstract reasoning concerning quantity or number? No. Does it contain any experimental reasoning concerning matter of fact and existence? No. Commit it then to the flames: for it can contain nothing but sophistry and illusion."

The Problem of Induction

One of Hume's most important contributions to philosophy was the identification of the so-called Problem of Induction, which has plagued, puzzled, and perplexed philosophers ever since.

Induction is a type of reasoning whereby general conclusions are drawn from specific observations. For example, after observing a large number of swans, all of them white, inductive reasoning might lead us to conclude that all swans are white. Induction also allows us to predict future events based on past experiences. For example, in the past, the sun has risen every morning; therefore we can predict that it will rise again tomorrow.

Without induction, we couldn't conduct our everyday lives. We would have no reason to expect food to nourish us, water to quench our thirst, or fire to burn us.

But, however essential it is, induction is not 100 percent reliable. We may have observed any number of white swans, but that doesn't guarantee there are no black ones. The sun may have risen on every previous morning, but that doesn't prove that it will rise tomorrow.

The problem with induction is that it takes for granted that the future will resemble the past. But we have no guarantee of this. Certainly, we believe it will. But we cannot justify our belief by any reasoned argument.

People sometimes try to justify induction by appealing to the fact that it has always worked in the past. But this is begging the question. You can't justify the belief that the future will resemble the past simply by pointing out that it has always done so in the past!

Indoor Ornithology

This paradox was devised by the German-born philosopher of science Carl Gustav Hempel (1905–1997). It goes by various names including Hempel's Paradox, the Paradox of the Ravens, and the Paradox of the Crows.

Counting Crows

A scientist, Martha, wishes to test the hypothesis "All crows are black." So off she goes, in search of crows. Every time she finds one, and confirms that it is indeed black, she feels a little more certain that her hypothesis is correct. This is standard inductive reasoning (see p. 29).

Each sighting of a black crow is what scientists call a confirming instance of Martha's hypothesis. The more confirming instances there are, the more probable the hypothesis becomes (provided, of course, that no blue, green, yellow, or white crows throw a wrench in the works).

Now things get interesting.

Indoor Ornithology

The statement "All crows are black" is logically equivalent to the statement "All non-black things are non-crows." In other words, both statements say precisely the same thing, albeit in different ways.

Thus, every confirming instance of "All non-black things are non-crows" must also count as a confirming instance of "All crows are black." This seemingly innocuous fact has some perplexing consequences, as the following example makes clear.

A blue pen is both non-black and a non-crow. So it counts as a confirming instance of "All non-black things are non-crows."

But this means that it is also a confirming instance of "All crows are black."

This is good news for Martha, the scientist. On rainy days she can carry out her ornithological research without leaving the comfort of her office. The blue pen on her desk confirms that all crows are black; as do the silver paperclip, the white writing paper, the yellow pencil, and the transparent plastic ruler.

The Paradox of the Crows

This, then, is the paradox. A blue pen confirms that "All non-black things are non-crows," and therefore confirms the logically equivalent "All crows are black." But this is absurd. How can a blue pen possibly lend weight to a hypothesis concerning the color of crows?

Thus, inductive reasoning embroils us in a paradox, highlighting once again the problem of induction.

One popular response is to insist that every non-black non-crow does confirm the hypothesis "All crows are black"; it is just that the degree of confirmation is very, very small, since the number of non-black objects vastly outweighs the number of crows.

Perhaps there is something in this response. It is certainly true that if we were to examine every non-black object in the world, and confirm that they are all non-

QUESTIONS TO CONSIDER

Consider the following scenario. Martha is outside conducting research. She comes across a murder of crows and is horrified to observe a white crow-like bird among them. With trembling fingers, she raises her binoculars, focuses on the bird, and is relieved to find that it is not a crow at all, but another, similar-sized, bird.

• Why is the solitary white bird more important to Martha's research than all of the accompanying black crows?

• Does Martha's discovery that the non-black bird is a non-crow help to confirm her hypothesis that all crows are black?

crows, we would have conclusive proof that all crows are black.

Non-Confirming Instances

One lesson we might draw from this discussion is that justifying a hypothesis involves more than simply piling up confirming instances. Background knowledge must guide our observations too.

For example, no one would take Martha's hypothesis seriously if it were based only on observations made within a short distance of her home. To be credible, her research must take into account that there are many different species of crow, in many different parts of the world, any of which may have adapted differently to their environments.

If there were such a thing as an Arctic crow (which there isn't), we might reasonably expect it to be white. In which case, in order to confirm her hypothesis that all crows are black, wouldn't Martha need to travel to the Arctic in search of non-confirming instances?

A Grue-some Problem

As we saw earlier in the chapter, induction is a type of reasoning whereby general conclusions are drawn from specific observations. However, as we also saw earlier, induction can be fallible, and here is another problem with inductive reasoning.

Science and Induction

Scientists rely on induction to formulate their theories. In fact, there could be no science without it. For example, it has been observed in countless instances that a test tube full of hydrogen will burn with a "squeaky pop." This allows us to formulate the general rule, "Hydrogen burns with a squeaky pop"—which is the standard lab test for hydrogen.

But induction is by no means infallible, as evidenced by the Problem of Induction (see p. 29) and the Paradox of the Crows (see pp. 30–31). In addition—as though it were not already beleaguered enough—poor old induction has to contend with a third challenge. This one was raised by the American philosopher Nelson Goodman (1906–1998), and is known as the New Riddle of Induction or, simply, the Grue Paradox.

Emeralds: Green or Grue?

Grue is a made-up word. Here's how it's defined: something is grue if 1) it is examined before 2020 and found to be green, or 2) it is not examined before 2020 and is blue.

Now, let's say that before 2020 we examine many, many emeralds and find them all to be green. These observations confirm the hypothesis that all emeralds are green. So we can predict that any emerald discovered after 2020 will be green.

But the same observations confirm the hypothesis that all emeralds are grue. So we can predict that any emerald discovered after 2020 will look blue.

This, then, is the problem: we can use inductive reasoning to predict that emeralds discovered after 2020 will be green; and we can use inductive reasoning to predict that emeralds discovered after 2020 will appear blue.

So, on top of Hume's traditional problem of induction we now have Goodman's New Riddle of Induction, which demonstrates that we can use inductive reasoning to make entirely different predictions based on the same evidence.

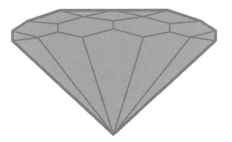
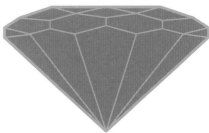

What's the Matter with Grue?

The green/grue hypotheses can't both be correct. We can't say "All emeralds are green" and "All emeralds are grue."

Clearly, the green hypothesis is the reasonable one. It would be insane to prefer the grue hypothesis. But why? What makes it OK to argue, "All examined emeralds are green, therefore all emeralds are green," while arguing that "All examined emeralds are grue, therefore all emeralds are grue," seems ridiculous? Think about this before reading on.

A commonsense response to Goodman's riddle might be to protest that grue is simply a made-up word—an artificial, unwieldy, and frankly rather silly cobbling together of the concepts blue and green. This being the case, nobody ever would form the hypothesis that "All emeralds are grue."

Green, like blue, is a basic property that everyone (at least, everyone with normal eyesight) knows and understands. Therefore it makes sense to use it when forming generalizations and making predictions about the world.

Grue, on the other hand, is not something that would ever enter into our hypotheses, because we have no reason for supposing that grueness is a feature of the world we inhabit.

Philosophers sometimes use the term "natural kinds." A natural kind can refer to a grouping of things which is a natural grouping rather than an artificial one; or it can refer to a common feature of things that can be used to make such natural groupings. Thus green and blue are natural kinds, whereas grue is not.

So perhaps we can resolve the Grue Paradox by insisting that scientific induction is only appropriate when applied to natural kinds.

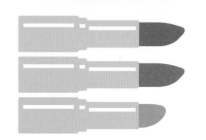

Exercise 1

Paradox of the Parlor

THE PROBLEM:

Agnes, Beatrice, and Chloe run a 24-hour beauty parlor. At least one of the three partners has to be there at all times. However, Beatrice only works with Agnes, and Chloe never works without one of the other two. Chloe complains that she always has to work. But her reasoning is bad. Actually, it is poor Agnes who can't get away. First try on your own to give a plausible-sounding argument to show that Chloe must always be at work in the parlor, but then show where the argument goes wrong; that is, use logic to free Chloe. Finally, prove that Agnes, like a prisoner, has to be there at all times.

THE METHOD:

Chloe might reason as follows to support her complaint. See if you can spot the error in her argument.

Chloe is aware that at least one of the partners must be working at all times. So she notes that if she is away from work, then if Agnes is away, Beatrice must stay to work. But Beatrice only works with Agnes, so if Agnes is away, Beatrice will be away. "If I am away from work," Chloe reasons, "there will be logical problems; because if Agnes is away, Beatrice must both stay and go. She has to stay because someone must if the two of us are away, and she has to go because she won't work without Agnes."

Chloe's reasoning has the following form.

If Chloe is away, then if Agnes is away, Beatrice must be working. (Someone has to stay.)

If Agnes is away, Beatrice is away. (Beatrice only works with Agnes.)

If we let C=Chloe is away from work, A=Agnes is away from work, and B=Beatrice is away from work (so that not-B=Beatrice is at work), then we have

If C, then if A, not-B.
If A, then B.

The appearance of contradiction arises if Agnes is away (A), for then it seems that

Beatrice must work and must also be away from work, which is not possible. This at least is the logical problem Chloe is trying to solve by inferring she will have to work.

However, it is also clear that, if Agnes stays to work, both Beatrice and Chloe can go away, so Chloe's reasoning is mistaken. She can indeed get away, if Agnes stays. The logical point Chloe missed is that the following propositions, however unusual, do not logically contradict each other, and both can be true:

> **If A, not-B.**
> **If A, then B.**

For instance, consider Albert, who dearly wants to join a softball team. But he will only join if the team makes him captain. So we have:

> **If Albert joins the team,**
> **he will be captain.**

Meanwhile, the team has decided to invite him to join on condition that he is not made captain. So we have:

> **If Albert joins the team,**
> **he will not be captain.**

There is nothing wrong with both these conditional statements being true, as long as Albert does not join the team. Indeed, the only way for both these statements to be true is for Albert not to join the team. The two statements, taken together as true, constitute logical proof that Albert won't join the softball team (for he can't, on pain of contradiction).

THE SOLUTION:

Just as Albert can't join the team, Agnes can't get away from work. Recall:

At least one of the partners must be working at all times.

Beatrice never works without Agnes.

Chloe never works without one of the other two.

It is easy to see that Agnes must always be at work. If Beatrice is working, so is Agnes. If Beatrice is not working, Chloe won't work unless Agnes does. So whether Beatrice is working or not, Agnes must.

Looked at differently, Chloe too is either working or not working. If Chloe is working, either Agnes or Beatrice must work with her, but Beatrice won't work without Agnes, so Agnes must stay too. If, on the other hand, Chloe is not working, then one of the other two must work; but Beatrice won't work alone, so Agnes is stuck again.

Agnes's choices are to work alone, to work with Beatrice, or to work with Chloe and Beatrice. She can't choose to not work, because then Beatrice won't, and then Chloe won't unless Beatrice does.

Chapter 2

Vagueness and Identity

To know what something is, it helps to know what it is not. But what do we do when it is hard to tell the two apart, as when entities change slowly but utterly, or when their boundaries are indistinct? Are the vague objects only vague language? There are heaps of classic paradoxes: a bald man with some hair, some children with muddy faces. Whether you are vague about identity, or identify with vagueness, you will definitely discover distinctive definitions of the indistinct in this chapter.

The Ship of Theseus: Part 1

Everyone knows the legend of Theseus, the Athenian youth who sailed to Crete, descended into the labyrinth, and slew the Minotaur. According to the Greek historian Plutarch, the Athenians preserved Theseus's ship for posterity. As time passed, any rotting or decaying planks were replaced with new timber in order to keep the ship in good repair. This led to a dispute among philosophers as to whether or not the repaired vessel ought to be regarded as the same as the original.

One might wonder why the Greek intellectual elite would trouble themselves with this question at all. It's an entertaining enough puzzle, perhaps worthy of an idle hour's speculation, but one that hardly seems to merit serious attention.

However, there's more to it than meets the eye. Bigger issues are at stake than the historical status of a few wooden planks. The Ship of Theseus is a kind of philosophical parable. It raises important questions about everything that grows, decays, or changes over time.

The Example of You

A more familiar example of this kind of question is pondered by people every day. For example, my wife Wendy has more than once remarked, when talking about her childhood, "I've changed so much, I sometimes wonder if I'm still the same person."

She has a point. Human cells don't last a lifetime. The body is constantly regenerating itself. Some cells last longer than others: the gut lining is replaced every five days; red blood cells every 120 days; and bones every 10 years. This means that, physically at least, little of childhood-Wendy has survived into adult-Wendy. So

in what sense can she be regarded as the same person?

The analogy with the Ship of Theseus is clear. In Wendy's case, cells are replaced rather than wooden planks, but similar principles apply.

The Ship of Theseus: Puzzle No. 1

Consider the point in time at which just one or two planks from Theseus's original ship have been replaced. At this stage it seems natural to regard the repaired ship as the original.

But then consider a later point, by which time the Athenians have made so many repairs that none of the original material remains. Can we still regard the repaired ship as the same vessel?

If we answer yes, we have a problem. Although the ship has changed gradually and incrementally, it has, nonetheless, changed totally. Not one part of the original vessel remains. And if no part of an entity survives, can the entity itself still remain?

If, on the other hand, we answer no, we have a different problem. Precisely when did the repaired ship cease to be the Ship of Theseus? Surely not when just one plank was replaced? Surely not two planks either. Where exactly do we draw the line?

Does the new ship come into being and the old ship disappear only when the very last plank is replaced?

Physical Continuity

We are faced with a dilemma. Whichever answer we give, we run into difficulties. But we can perhaps avoid the dilemma by appealing to the concept of physical continuity. Although every part of Theseus's ship has been replaced, the process has been gradual. The timber has been replaced piece by piece without ever compromising the vessel's overall structure. This smooth, unbroken transition seems sufficient to preserve the identity of the ship throughout all of the changes.

On the basis of physical continuity, then, we can assert that the much-repaired ship is indeed still the Ship of Theseus.

SOMETHING TO THINK ABOUT

Although most of the human body's cells are replaced over time, there are exceptions. For example, the cerebral cortex of the brain does not regenerate. Its cells are as old as we are. The cerebral cortex plays a key role in consciousness, memory, perception, thought, and language.

Does this have any bearing upon Wendy's question about whether she is still the same person as she was during childhood?

ANSWERS

Quite possibly. Physically, a small portion of child-Wendy remains in adult-Wendy. Furthermore, the cerebral cortex is perhaps the most important part of us as far as self-identity is concerned. So its survival into adulthood may have a special significance.

The Ship of Theseus: Part 2

If we accept that physical continuity allows objects to preserve their identity while undergoing changes, we have a solution to the first puzzle regarding the Ship of Theseus. Even if every single plank on Theseus's ship is replaced, we are still left with the same vessel.

The Ship of Theseus: Puzzle No. 2

Now consider a more complicated scenario in which the rotting planks are gradually replaced by new ones, as before, but are then used to construct a replica vessel somewhere else.

There are now two ships, which we can label A and B. Ship A is constituted from new timber which has gradually replaced the old. Ship B has been constructed from the original planks—and to the original specifications—but in an entirely different location. Which is the genuine article?

Ship A has a valid claim to being the Ship of Theseus. After all, it is identical in every respect to the ship constituted from replacement parts in Puzzle No. 1. Physical continuity has been preserved throughout all the changes, thereby preserving the identity of the original ship.

However, ship B has an equally valid claim to being the Ship of Theseus. After all, it is made of precisely the same material as the original, put together in precisely the same way.

Imagine an archaeologist discovering the location of Noah's Ark. She digs it up, dismantles it, and then reassembles it in a museum gallery. No one would deny that the boat in the museum is Noah's Ark, merely because it has been taken apart and put together again. Yet this is precisely the process that has taken place with regard to ship B. Therefore ship B is the Ship of Theseus.

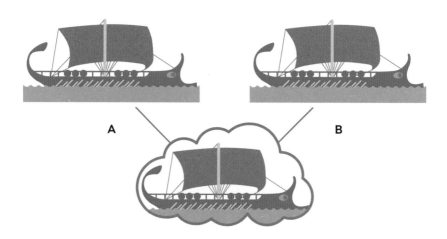

A   B

A REAL-LIFE EXAMPLE

Before writing this book I visited the Golden Pavilion in Kyoto—one of Japan's most celebrated pieces of architecture. It's an elegant, three-story wooden building, covered in gold, and situated beside a picturesque ornamental lake.

Originally constructed in 1397, the temple has burned down and been rebuilt several times, most recently in the 1950s. Upon hearing this, I, like many Western visitors, felt a little cheated. I was disappointed not to be seeing the "real" thing. However, the Japanese seem to have no problem accepting the current building as the genuine article.

The Golden Pavilion suffers from even worse identity problems than the Ship of Theseus. The new building does not have the same material constitution as the old, nor can it boast physical continuity. In this case, does it have any claim to authenticity?

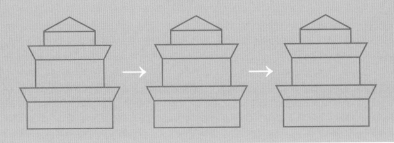

The Paradox

Here, then, is the paradox. There are two ships, A and B. Valid reasoning leads to the conclusion that ship A is the Ship of Theseus. Equally valid reasoning leads to the conclusion that ship B is the Ship of Theseus. But surely there can only be one Ship of Theseus?

Ship A's claim is based on physical continuity. A series of smooth, gradual transitions lead from the original vessel to ship A. Ship B's claim is based on material constitution. It is made from precisely the same stuff, put together in precisely the same way as the original.

A Matter of Context?

Perhaps ultimately it is just a matter of context. In some situations it makes sense to view ship A as the Ship of Theseus; in other situations, ship B. Or maybe this is simply ducking the question. Perhaps we ought to decide which of the two criteria, physical continuity or material constitution, takes precedence for objects of this kind. This is explored further in another famous paradox, the River of Heraclitus (see pp. 46–47).

Psychological Continuity

The problem posed by Theseus's ship concerns the physical identity of an object. However, we can also of course consider identity in relation to human beings—what's commonly termed *personal identity*. Here, physical continuity doesn't seem so important—the fact that your cells change over time, you lose a limb or gain an artificial one—because what's important here is your mind: you are the same person over time because the consciousness that's aware of what you're doing now also remembers what it did in the past. The English philosopher John Locke was the first to propose memory as the basis for this continuity, but, as various critics have pointed out, the matter is not so simple.

The first to object to Locke's proposition was the Scottish philosopher Thomas Reid. Imagine, he said, that a young boy steals some apples from an orchard. The boy grows up to be a soldier, who during a battle captures the enemy's flag. As an old man, the soldier becomes a general. And here's the problem: while the general can remember being the soldier who captured the flag, he can no longer remember being the boy who stole the apples. So, according to Locke's criteria, the general is the same person as the soldier, but not the same as the boy (because he no longer possesses the boy's memories). And yet, Reid points out, this is paradoxical: the soldier is the same person as the boy because he can remember stealing the apples, and the general is the same person as the soldier because he remembers stealing the flag. Logic therefore dictates that if the general is the same person as the soldier, and the soldier is the same person as the boy, then the general is the same person as the boy. Reid's point is that memory can't be a criterion for identity because it results in paradox.

A Chain of Memories

The English philosopher Derek Parfit tried to rescue Locke's theory by suggesting that perhaps all that's required are overlapping links in the chain of memory: perhaps you can't remember what you did ten days ago, but you would have remembered that nine days ago; and eight days ago you would have remembered what you did nine days ago . . . and so on. And, by this method, we can show that the general is the same person as the boy.

Implanted Memories

However, there's another, deeper problem, first pointed out by Bishop Joseph Butler. If I say that I am the same person as I was last year, because I have that person's memories, then I'm in fact assuming that those are "my" memories. This seems an odd thing to say, but it's a fair point: Locke's theory assumes what it wants to prove. Let's illustrate this using an example from science fiction. In Philip K. Dick's short story, "We Can Remember It for You Wholesale" (later filmed as *Total Recall*), unable to afford a real holiday

WAR CRIMES

Memory is a central strut of personal identity, but also of moral culpability. In order to plead guilty to a crime (and thereby, perhaps, receive a lesser sentence for admission of guilt), a person must be able to remember committing the crime in question.

But what if, due to intoxication or some other cause of amnesia, this is not the case?

This was in fact the alleged situation concerning Rudolf Hess, former deputy to Adolf Hitler, when standing trial for war crimes at Nuremberg. Hess claimed no memory of key events, but was deemed otherwise mentally fit.

For such reasons, certain courts now allow what is termed a *Norgaard Plea*, where a defendant claiming not to remember committing the crime with which he is charged, but for which there is sufficient evidence to convict, may nonetheless plead guilty (and thus avail himself of a plea deal).

to Mars, a man purchases artificial memories of a such a trip, which—to give an exciting twist—are constructed as the memories of a secret agent. However, the process of implanting the memories unlocks the subject's apparently hidden memories . . . of being a secret agent on Mars. Now, is he *actually* a secret agent, or is this just the result of the implantation process? He cannot appeal to "what he really remembers," because that is the very question at stake: are these his real memories?

Reid's point can probably be made with more mundane scenarios, but it nonetheless reveals that using memory to establish personal identity is problematic.

The Teletransportation Paradox

In trying to establish a basis for personal identity based on memory, Parfit ends up by proposing that, in fact, there may be hypothetical situations whereby a person might survive, but where personal identity was not maintained. But how can that be? Doesn't your continued existence guarantee that the person who survives is "you"?

The basis of this seeming paradox is Parfit's famous thought experiment involving a teletransporter—that is, the sort of "transporter" that we find in *Star Trek* and other science fiction, whereby physical objects are "beamed" from one location to another. Imagine, says Parfit, that you use one such device to travel to Mars. The way Parfit's transporter works is to copy all the information related to each and every particle making up your physical body, before transmitting it to Mars, where it will be used to reassemble "you" out of particles there. Since (for the purposes of this argument) "you" are simply a certain configuration of atoms (including your brain states and memories), then the person who ends up on Mars will have as good a claim to be "you" as you yourself do. Once the copy is made, your original body is then destroyed.

Which Is The "Real" You?

In this case, Parfit argues, you have both survival and personal identity: the "you" on Mars is still you. However, now imagine that the transporter malfunctions, and instead of destroying your original body, it merely fatally damages it. In that situation, the paradox then is this: "you" exist, but you are no longer unique. As you die on Earth, should you nonetheless be consoled that "you" will live on? Or should you mourn your imminent death?

You and Your Martian Twin

Parfit argues that you should in fact be consoled by your Martian twin's continued existence. He is able to do this because he believes that a person is simply a certain relation of experiences, memories, habits, preferences, beliefs and other qualities. As long as the twin contains enough of those experiences and qualities, connected together in a certain way, then the person they make up lives on. For Parfit, it doesn't even matter that there is not direct continuity between the old and new body (it is made up of different atoms), for it is the pattern of memory and experience that is important—that is what you really are. The fact that the transporter accident may result in the loss of the notion that each of us is unique is also irrelevant, because what we gain is a certain sort of immortality. In fact, Parfit thinks, this is true anyway, for long after both you and your Martian twin are dead there is a sense in which "you" will live on: in the memories that others hold of you; in the words, images, and possessions that you leave behind, and the effects these have on other conscious beings; in the consequences of your actions, the schemes, and plans that you set in motion while alive, and which continue to ripple outward after you are gone.

The Entire History of You

But would this really matter to you? Let's say that after you die someone takes all your social media profiles—your Facebook posts and tweets, your Instagram photos, all the likes and shares—and uses this to inform an AI programmed to interact with others. Could such a thing ever be considered "you"? If the research was comprehensive enough, the AI sophisticated enough (such AI "bots" are now quite common, and will only improve), wouldn't this be equivalent to what Parfit is proposing? So, are you happy for your AI twin? No?

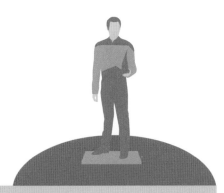

RESURRECTION

Obviously, survival after death is not just a problem for sci-fi scenarios such as Parfit's teletransporter example, but has a long history in religious literature. For instance, certain Christians interpret the doctrine of Resurrection in physical terms—that is, that God will resurrect the faithful *in their physical bodies*. But will they be the *same* bodies? And what would that mean? That God would have to resurrect an individual's body out of the *same atoms*? But atoms swap and change over time, and being the same person requires more than merely possessing the same atoms, doesn't it?

Perhaps it is a matter of possessing the same features or qualities, then? But that's problematic, too, for the same person can be radically different over time.

The obvious religious solution would be to consider a person not as their body, but as their soul. But that has its problems, too.

The River of Heraclitus

"It is in changing that things find repose."
—Heraclitus, ca. 500 BCE

Heraclitus was one of the earliest philosophers. He lived in Ephesus, Asia Minor, around 500 BCE. Little is known for certain about his life, but he seems to have been something of a misanthrope. He displayed a contemptuous attitude toward his fellows, regarding most of them as unthinking fools. His misanthropy may even have led to his early death. He is said to have developed dropsy after removing himself from society and living off grass and plants.

Heraclitus wrote just one book, which was notoriously difficult and obscure. After reading it, Socrates reportedly commented, "What I understand is splendid; and so too, I'm sure, is what I don't understand." The book survives only in fragments, some of which are of dubious authenticity.

According to Heraclitus, the world is in a permanent state of flux. Everything is constantly changing. He identified fire as nature's basic element: a suitably unstable substance to account for a continually changing universe.

Heraclitus's Paradox

In his philosophical dialogue, *Cratylus*, Plato quotes Heraclitus as saying that "You cannot step into the same river twice." This seems absurd. After all, we patently can step twice into the same river. We simply have to enter it on two separate occasions—say, Monday and Tuesday.

The problem is that rivers are made of flowing water; and the water that makes up the river on Monday is different from the water that makes up the river on Tuesday. Therefore, since the river is water, and since the water does not stay the same, Monday's river is not identical to Tuesday's.

Even worse, the river may undergo dramatic changes between one day and the next. It may burst its banks, change course, or even dry up completely. In such cases, not only will the river's material constitution change (as is the case with the Ship of Theseus on pp. 38–41), but also its overall structure. By this account, on consecutive occasions we step into very different rivers.

The paradox, then, is that we both can and cannot step twice into the same river. Or, as it is more poetically expressed in

$$\chi = \zeta = \chi = \phi = \chi = \psi$$

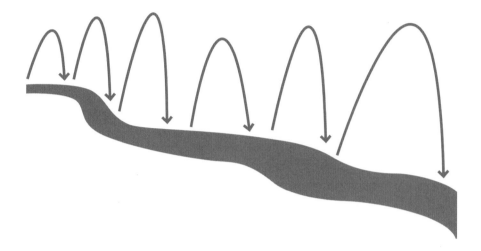

one of Heraclitus's fragments: "Into the same river we do and do not step."

Resolving the Paradox

Perhaps there is no real paradox here. Maybe it is just a matter of context. If, by a river, we mean a body of water taking a certain course toward the sea, then obviously we can step twice into the same river. But if we mean a very specific body of water, where each H_2O molecule is essential to its identity, then of course we cannot.

Alternatively, we can try to resolve Heraclitus's paradox by appealing once again to the concept of physical continuity (as described on p. 39). Although the material constitution of the river changes moment by moment, it does so smoothly and gradually. There is a connectedness that links each successive temporal phase of the river. Perhaps this is sufficient to preserve its identity.

Learning from Heraclitus

But perhaps the best insight to be gained from this paradox comes from Heraclitus himself. One of his most celebrated philosophical ideas is the doctrine of universal flux, which holds that everything is constantly changing; nothing stays the same.

The River of Heraclitus provides us with a perfect illustration of this concept. Change is part and parcel of a river's identity. In fact, a river remains what it is only by changing what it contains. This insight may shed light on another of Heraclitus's fragments: "On those stepping into rivers staying the same other and other waters flow."

Perhaps the true lesson to be learned is that some existents (maybe all of them, if Heraclitus is right) are defined by change. Change does not destroy their identity; it is an essential feature of it.

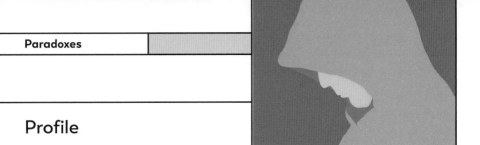

Profile

Eubulides

Eubulides was a Greek philosopher from the fourth century BCE who invented a number of ingenious paradoxes. Little is known about his life, and what we do know comes to us mostly from the writings of Diogenes Laertius, who tells us that he was a student of Euclides, who was himself a pupil of Socrates.

A contemporary of Aristotle, Eubulides did not see eye-to-eye with his countryman, either philosophically or personally. Some sources even claim that Eubulides went so far as to engage in a character-assassination of Aristotle, accusing him of spying on the Athenians on behalf of the Macedonians.

Be that as it may, Diogenes Laertius credits Eubulides with seven paradoxes: the Hooded Man, the Elektra, the Disguised, the Horns, the Liar, the Heap, and the Bald Man.

In ancient times these paradoxes were often dismissed as trivial and unimportant. His rival Aristotle briefly discusses and tersely dismisses them. Cicero describes them as "far-fetched and pointed sophisms." And Seneca acidly comments, "Not to know them does no harm; and mastering them does no good."

But Eubulides had the last laugh. His paradoxes have stood the test of time, and are still debated by philosophers and logicians today. The Heap, the Bald Man, and the Liar are considered particularly important.

These are the paradoxes attributed to Eubulides by Diogenes Laertius.

The Hooded Man
You say you know your brother. Yet when your brother is hooded you are unable to identify him. So you both do and do not know your brother.

The Elektra
Elektra was raised separately from her brother, Orestes, but she knows that Orestes is her brother. When he is introduced to her as a stranger, does she know her brother, Orestes?

We cannot answer no, since Elektra knows that Orestes is her brother. We cannot answer yes, because Elektra does not know that the man standing before her is Orestes.

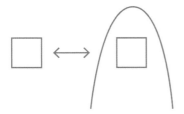

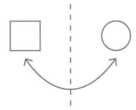

The Disguised

This paradox is merely a variation on the Hooded Man and the Elektra.

The Horns

Suppose someone asks, "Have you lost your horns?" How do you reply? If you answer no, then presumably you still have them. If you answer yes, then presumably you once had them.

Alternatively: What you have not lost, you still have. But you have not lost your horns. Therefore you still have them.

The Liar

If I say, "What I am now saying is false," am I telling the truth? This is one of the trickiest and most important paradoxes ever devised. It is discussed on pp. 72–73.

The Heap

This is another fiendishly difficult and very important paradox, in which Eubulides demonstrates that a single grain of sand constitutes a heap. It is discussed on pp. 50–51.

The Bald Man

This celebrated paradox is very similar to the Heap. It is also discussed on pp. 50–51.

A CHALLENGE

Try to resolve the Hooded Man, the Elektra, and the Horns paradoxes.

HINTS

The Hooded Man and the Elektra are similar. They rely on the ambiguity of the verb "to know." That is, we can know someone both in the sense of being acquainted with them; and in the sense of recognizing them.

Meanwhile, the Horns paradox begins with a loaded question: "Have you lost your horns?" This presupposes that you once had them. So is a simple "yes" or "no" really an appropriate response?

The Bald Man and the Heap

Introduced on the previous page, the paradoxes of the Bald Man and the Heap are two of Eubulides's most celebrated problems.

The Bald Man

A man with a full head of hair is clearly not bald. Furthermore, losing a single hair will not make him bald. In fact, the loss of a single hair can never turn a non-bald man into a bald one. So no one can ever become bald.

The Heap

A million grains of sand piled together make a heap. If a single grain is removed, the heap remains. In fact, the loss of a single grain can never turn a heap into a non-heap. However, the continual removal of single grains will eventually leave just one grain remaining. So a solitary grain of sand is a heap.

The Bald Man and the Heap have a very similar logical structure. They are often referred to as "sorites paradoxes" (from the Greek word soros meaning "heap") and are also sometimes described as "little-by-little" arguments.

Sorites paradoxes have puzzled, intrigued, and infuriated philosophers for more than two thousand years. So it's fair to say that they don't admit of an easy solution. Some attempted resolutions are discussed on pp. 54–55.

In the meantime, here are two similar-looking puzzles that are perfectly solvable. See if you can spot the flaws in these little-by-little arguments.

FREEZING POINT

A temperature of a thousand degrees is above freezing point. A temperature that is just a single degree lower is still above freezing point. In fact, a drop of just one degree can never bring a temperature down below freezing point. So no temperature can ever drop below freezing point.

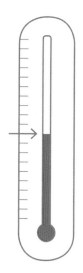

SOLUTION

This argument is clearly flawed. There is a very definite temperature at which water freezes: 32°F/0°C. So it is wrong to claim that "A drop of just one degree can never bring the temperature down below freezing point."

Contrast this with the Bald Man and the Heap, where there is no clear cut-off between the states of bald and non-bald and being a heap or not a heap.

ALL HORSES ARE THE SAME COLOR

Imagine putting together a group of horses, taken at random. The group can be any size: say ten. Is it possible to construct a proof that all ten horses are the same color?

We could indeed construct such a proof, if only we could prove that any group of nine horses are the same color. In that case, we could partition off any nine horses from our group of ten, and know that they are the same color. Therefore all ten must be the same.

But is there any way to prove that any group of nine horses are all the same color? Yes, provided we can prove

that any eight horses are the same. And this, in turn, can be proved provided we can show that any group of seven horses are the same color. And so on and so on, all the way down through six, five, four, three, two, and one.

But in any group containing just one horse, clearly every horse is the same color. Therefore, by this chain of reasoning, we have established that any ten horses must be the same color.

Of course, we could have begun this argument with a group of any size. Therefore all horses are the same color!

SOLUTION

We can indeed prove that any ten horses are the same color provided we can show that any nine horses are the same color. This holds true as we count down through eight, seven, six, five, four, and three. But eight, seven, six, five, four, and three. But the proof breaks down once we reach two horses. The fact that any one horse must be identical in color to itself by no means guarantees that any two horses are the same color.

Vagueness

At the heart of the paradoxes of the Bald Man and the Heap lies the concept of vagueness. The Bald Man relies upon the vagueness of the word "bald"; and the Heap relies upon the vagueness of the word "heap."

The problem, insofar as the Bald Man is concerned, is that there is no sharp cut-off point between what does and does not count as "bald." We can see that the word applies to someone with few hairs, and does not apply to someone with a full head of hair. However, there are borderline cases where we simply cannot tell whether it applies or not.

Similarly, there is no sharp cut-off point that separates heaps from non-heaps. Again we are confronted by borderline cases where we cannot tell whether the word "heap" applies or not. These borderline cases are what give sorites paradoxes their bite.

This is why the Freezing Point Puzzle (see p. 50) never gets off the ground. "Freezing point" is a precise term, not a vague one. Once water drops to 32°F/0°C it has reached freezing point. There are no borderline cases, at least in principle.

Inquiry Resistance

The vagueness of words like "bald" and "heap" cannot be done away with by any amount of information-gathering. Even if we know the precise number of hairs on a man's head, we may still not know whether to call him bald. Even if we count grains of sand down to the very last grain, we may still not know whether they constitute a heap.

Thus, vagueness is said to be "inquiry resistant." When it comes to borderline cases of words like "bald" or "heap" there is simply no way to settle the issue. However carefully we count, or however accurately we measure, the vagueness remains. It is inherent in the words themselves.

More Vague Words

There are many vague words besides "bald" and "heap." Consider the following: tall, rich, child, clever, small, and old.

WHEN IS A DOOR NOT A DOOR?

It is easy to spot the vagueness inherent in words like tall, rich, child, clever, small, and old. But even words that appear precise may turn out to be infected with vagueness upon closer inspection. See if you can identify any vagueness in the following words: chair, person, good, book, father.

HINT

Try to think of borderline cases where it is unclear whether or not the given word ought to apply. For example, does the word "person" apply to a fetus? If so, at what point in its development? If you shave some wood off a chair, is it still a chair? Just how much wood can you shave off before the word "chair" no longer applies?

BUILD YOUR OWN PARADOX

"Small" is a vague word. So it should be possible to use it to construct a sorites paradox. Try proving that all numbers are small.

SOLUTION

Something like this would do the trick: One is a small number. Add one and you still have a small number. In fact, adding just one can never turn a small number into a large one. But by continually adding one you can eventually reach any number. Therefore all numbers are small.

What height must someone reach in order to be tall? How much money does it take to be rich? At what age do you stop being a child? And so on. All of these words are vague since they all admit of borderline cases. We could construct sorites-type paradoxes for all of them, and for many other words besides.

Vagueness Matters

There is more to vagueness than mere philosophical hair-splitting. A number of important ethical problems are fueled, at least in part, by the vagueness inherent in certain words. For example, some of the debate on the rights and wrongs of abortion centers upon the issue of when a fetus becomes a "person." Similarly, debate about the appropriate age for sexual consent is very much tied in to the notion of when a "child" becomes an "adult."

Resolving the Sorites

There must be something wrong with the arguments presented in the Bald Man and the Heap. We know this because their conclusions (no one can ever become bald; a solitary grain of sand is a heap) are clearly absurd. But identifying precisely what is wrong is another matter.

At this point, it will be helpful to outline the logical structure of sorites paradoxes, using the Heap as an example.

1. 1,000,000 grains of sand piled up together make a heap.
2. If 1,000,000 grains of sand make a heap then so do 999,999.
3. But if 999,999 grains make a heap then so do 999,998.
4. But if 999,998 grains make a heap then so do 999,997 … and so on.
5. So 1 grain of sand is a heap.

This can be put more succinctly:

1. 1,000,000 grains of sand piled up together make a heap.
2. If n grains make a heap then so do $n{-}1$ grains.
3. So 1 grain of sand is a heap.

Expressing the argument in this precise manner brings out a key feature of sorites paradoxes, namely that vague words like "heap" are tolerant of small changes. The difference of a single grain is not sufficient to turn a heap into non-heap, just as the difference of a single hair cannot turn a non-bald man into a bald one.

But here's the rub. Small changes cannot turn heaps into non-heaps or bald men into non-bald, but big changes can. And yet big changes come about simply through the accumulation of small ones. Thus, small changes both do and do not make heaps into non-heaps, and hairy men into bald.

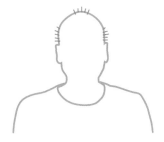

Resolving Sorites Paradoxes

The Bald Man and the Heap have proven to be fiendishly difficult puzzles. Philosophers and logicians are still debating them today, more than two thousand years after Eubulides first concocted them. Here are some possible approaches to resolving them:

Define Fixed Boundaries

Sorites paradoxes can be avoided if we define fixed boundaries for vague words like "bald" and "heap." For example, we could say that "heap" applies only to collections of more than, say, 10,000 grains, or that "bald" applies only to men with fewer than 1,000 hairs.

Deny Vagueness

Some philosophers claim that we do not need to define fixed boundaries for words like "bald" and "heap," because those boundaries already exist. According to the epistemic theory, vague words do draw sharp boundaries—it's just that we don't know where they are. By this account, there's a precise cut-off point at which a heap becomes a non-heap, and at which a hairy man becomes a bald one. Vagueness is not intrinsic to the words themselves. It boils down to our own ignorance.

> **TO THINK ABOUT...**
>
> Which of these approaches to resolving sorites paradoxes seems the most promising? Can you spot potential difficulties for any of them? For example, the first approach involves assigning fixed boundaries. But precisely where should these boundaries be? We don't know where heaps end and non-heaps begin, so won't any boundary be purely arbitrary? And if that is the case then what use is an arbitrary boundary?

Invoke "Degrees of Truth"

Assuming (contrary to the strategies of defining fixed boundaries or denying vagueness) that there are genuine borderline cases for vague words like "bald" and "heap," another tack is to suggest that not every proposition is either true or false, but that there are degrees of truth. By this account, it is true to say that a very large number of grains constitutes a heap; and it is false to say that a very small number of grains constitutes a heap. But for borderline cases, it is neither true nor false. The degree of truth decreases as the number of grains drops down toward the lower boundary of "heapness."

Exercise 2

Muddy Children

THE PROBLEM:

Some children assemble in an indefinitely large circle. Each child can see clearly the faces of all the other kids, though none can see its own. A teacher informs them that at least one among them has a muddy face, and asks any muddy-faced child to step forward into the circle. If there is no response, the question is repeated. The paradox: assuming *n* children with muddy faces, no child will step forward until the *n*-th request, and then all *n* children will step at once; but if instead the teacher—*without first having told the children* that one among them is muddy-faced—merely repeats the question as before, then no child will ever step forward. How can the teacher's telling them what they can already see for themselves make so big a difference?

THE METHOD:

To see the force of the paradox, it helps to appreciate the remarkable mental abilities of these imaginary children, who can each see all the faces of the other children, regardless of the size of the circle. In larger circles, such perceptive powers are superhuman, but let that be no objection. Also, the children are all immediately aware that every other child also sees every face but its own. What's more, as we shall see, the deductive powers of these children are presumed flawless, even when premises become inordinately long.

For instance, suppose the teacher has told them that there is at exactly one muddy face among them. The child with the muddy face will know theirs is the muddy one, since it can see every other child's face, and no child's face it sees is muddy; the muddy face must be the one face it cannot see: its own. If the muddy-faced child did not know that at least one face in the circle was muddy, it could not infer its own face was muddy, and would not step forward. In this important first case, on which all the others depend, the teacher's words make all the difference.

Now suppose that just two children have mud on their faces. Every child will have already seen for itself what the teacher says in advance, for they will see two muddy faces—except for the two children whose faces are muddy; but even they can see for themselves that at least one child's face is muddy, as teacher says. So, no child will step forward at the teacher's first request. Knowing that children cannot see their own faces, each child will infer that there must be more than one muddy face among them. To the clean-faced children, this is obvious, since they already see two muddy faces. But to those two who see only one muddy face, it only now becomes clear that there is more than one. For if there had been only one, he or she would have stepped forward at the first request. Since no child stepped forward earlier, it too must have seen a muddy face that was not its own. The two muddy-faced children now know that their face, too, is muddy, since each is aware that the muddy face seen by the one muddy-faced child it does see does not belong to anyone else in the circle. Both muddy-faced children make the same inference, and both step forward.

Had the teacher *not* told them beforehand that at least one of them was muddy-faced, none would ever be able to infer that their own face was muddy, despite plainly seeing for themselves what the teacher said. They can see it, but if the teacher doesn't say it, no child will step forward. Why?

THE SOLUTION:

If the teacher has not told them, then after the first request no child will step forward, even when there is only one muddy-faced child in the circle. At the second round, if there are two mud-faced children, they can no longer assume that, had there been only one mud-faced child in the circle, it would have stepped forward already. Without that assumption, self-identification as mud-faced in all later rounds is also impossible.

As we saw above in the two-muddy-faces scenario, the own-face conclusion of the two muddy-faced children depends upon an inference made after no child stepped forward upon the first request. By the time the second question is asked, the hypothesis that there is only one muddy face has been refuted. Of course, this was only tenable to the two mud-faced children, who saw one—and only one—face. What all the clean-faced kids knew just by looking, the two mud-faced kids realize only after there is no response from any visible mud-faced kids after the first request. Thus, by the time the second request begins, each child knows that there are at least two muddy faces.

The n children who have muddy faces know at once that there is *at most n* muddy faces, but they only learn that there are *at least n* when the $n-1$ mud-faced children they see do not step forward at the $n-1$th request. For the clean-faced children, the opposite is true: at the outset they can plainly see n mud-faced children, so they know there are *at least n* muddy faces (and *at most $n+1$*); but they only learn that there are *at most n* mud-faced children when the n they see step forward after the n-th request.

Chapter 3

Logic and Truth

If the truth will set you free, logic is the key. A fixed devotion to the truth and scrupulous logic can yet result in surprise and seeming contradiction. Again, we do not ask *What is true?*, but rather *What is truth? What does it even mean to say a proposition or belief is true?* We also look at linguistic reference, self-reference, set membership, and provability. The paradoxes here range from the frivolous to the quotidian, from linguistic to mathematical, but penetrate at times to central issues in philosophy and mathematical logic.

Paradoxes of Logic

Paradoxes of logic and truth can be both fun and infuriating at the same time, which is perhaps itself a paradox of sorts. So, before we delve deeper, here are a few light-hearted examples to consider.

The Visiting Card Paradox

Try this at your next cocktail party, but preferably not before your third martini. Hand someone a blank card and a pen, and ask them to hand the card back to you with a mark on it if—and only if—they think you will find it blank when you receive it from them. If they think you will find it blank, they should mark it; but then it won't be blank. If they think you will find a mark on it, they should leave it blank; but then you won't!

If you think this has you on the edge of losing your mind, then consider Ivan Pavlov's poor dogs. Pavlov famously trained his dogs to salivate at the mere sound of a bell by repeatedly pairing the bell with meat—an example of so-called classical conditioning. However, he carried this further, and with all his usual experimental rigor, he and his coinvestigators trained a dog to expect food at the presentation of a circle, but to expect no food at the presentation of an ellipse. Gradually they lessened the difference between the two shapes, until they became indistinguishable to the dog, which therefore had no idea what to expect. The cruel result was an induced psychosis, a psychological breakdown similar to what might be caused by thinking too hard about the Visiting Card Paradox.

Gallows Humor

A city in a strange land passed a law requiring all who would enter the city to state their business. Those who did so truthfully were permitted to enter and depart in peace. Those who uttered falsehoods were to be hanged upon a nearby gallows, which had been built for this sole purpose. A traveler came and was asked his business as he tried to enter the city. "My business in this city is simply to be hanged upon those gallows," he asserted.

According to the law of this land, should he be granted free entry or be hanged? If he told the truth, he has come to be hanged; unless he is held to that, he will not have been speaking truly, and so should be hanged. But if he is to be hanged, he has spoken truly, and should be free to enter and depart. (It takes a terrible cynic to suggest that he should be hanged, and then set free to go.)

A Lover's Logic

Desperate to prevail upon his beloved, a clever Lothario puts two questions to her:

i) Will you answer this question the way you answer my next question?

ii) Will you make passionate love with me?

The poor girl is in trouble however she answers the first question—assuming she must stay true to her answer. If she says yes, to keep her word, she must answer yes to the second. If she answers no, then to keep her word, she must answer the second question differently. Silence is probably her wisest reply, or perhaps laughter.

Is "No" Your Answer to This Question?

Here is an easy question that you will never answer correctly. The correct answer will be plain to anyone who hears your response, and they will easily be able to give it. But you will never be able to. If you say yes, then the correct answer is no; so you answer falsely. If your answer is no, then no is your answer, and the correct answer is yes. In either case you get it wrong.

The Airy Box

The British Astronomer Royal G. B. Airy (1801–1892) is said to have found an empty box at the Greenwich Observatory in London. Upon finding this he wrote "empty box" on a piece of paper and, somewhat perversely, put it inside.

It is passing strange that an explanatory note, intended to save one the labor of checking inside the box, should be placed there. One might more readily imagine an empty box with a label, which reads "This box is empty." Attached to the outside, such a label is true. Placed inside the box, it makes itself false. Alternatively, suppose the label says: "The box this label is inside is empty." Outside of any box, the subject of this sentence fails to refer—there is no box inside which the label is located. However, once inside an otherwise empty box, the sentence becomes false.

What happens if you now glue either of these labels, smoothly and securely, to the inside of an empty box? Is the box still empty? When the label goes from being the contents of the box to being part of its inside surface, does the sentence on it suddenly become true? Can this glue (which is also inside the box) make a difference to the veracity of the sentence?

Now suppose you find an empty box, open it, and upon its inside walls write, "This box is empty." Inside this box there are now ink, words, and a sentence. But, despite these additions, isn't it after all an empty box? Isn't the sentence true?

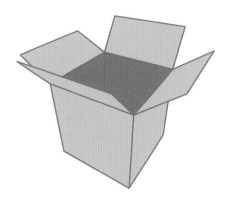

How to Expect the Unexpected

"Expect the unexpected" is a common piece of cautionary advice. In its everyday usage its meaning is something like, "Don't make too many assumptions" or "Be well prepared." However, what if we were to take it literally—is it really possible to expect something that we don't expect?

More Gallows Reasoning

A prisoner is sentenced on a Sunday to be hanged. The judge decrees that the hanging shall take place at noon on one of the next five days, but that the prisoner shall not know which. In effect, the judge sentences him to a surprise hanging. The quick-thinking prisoner protests that this is impossible, reasoning that it cannot be Friday, five days hence, because come Thursday afternoon he would be in a position to know, thereby ruining the surprise. Having ruled out Friday, he could go on to infer on Thursday morning that Thursday would have to be the day; so again he could not be surprised. Repeating this reasoning, he rules out the remaining three days. There shall be no surprise hanging, he bravely retorts.

Is this a genuine paradox? One in which unexceptionable premises lead by irrefutable reasoning to a wholly unacceptable conclusion? Ask yourself: Is this prisoner's conclusion unacceptable? Are his assumptions above reproach? Is his reasoning flawless? If all of these questions are answered affirmatively, the paradox is genuine. However, if even one of them must be answered in the negative, the paradox is merely apparent.

Testing, Testing ...

A less gruesome and more common version of this purported paradox is the surprise exam. A teacher announces that there will be a surprise exam in the next week. A clever student objects that this is impossible. The class meets once a day, Monday to Friday. On Thursday after class, if the exam has not already been given, all the students will know the exam will take place on Friday, the last chance that week. But then it will not be a surprise, so the teacher will have spoken falsely. If Friday is not a possible date for the surprise exam, that leaves the other four days; so by Wednesday after class, everyone will know that the exam will have to occur on Thursday, once more spoiling the surprise. In this way each day is ruled out and the element of surprise is lost.

Surprise, Surprise

The element of surprise, in examinations or hangings, is a sort of deception, a deception by omission. The prisoner is not told on what day the hanging will be, only given a finite window in which it will occur. A speaker risks being self-defeating by announcing a window in which a surprise will happen. The sense of paradox would evaporate if the judge were, more

PARADOX OF THE GRID

Imagine a closed room with a grid on the floor numbered as follows:

1	2	3
4	5	6
7	8	9

You are blindfolded with your arms tied. You know you are standing on some cell on this grid, but you don't know which. Your challenge is to find out where you are, but to do so you are allowed only two moves. A move entails stepping to a neighboring cell, either, up, down, left, or right. Attempting to do so and running into the outer wall instead also counts as a move. Your maniacal captor has told you that your task is impossible, that you are in a position undiscoverable in two moves.

Assuming this to be the case, you reason that you cannot be in any corner squares, since two moves will suffice to locate yourself. (Bumping into a wall while attempting to move upward and then again right, for instance, will prove that you are in square 3.) Since being in a corner square is discoverable in two moves, you can now go on to rule out the even-numbered squares. Clearly, moving once upward into a wall will now suffice to show that you are in square 2 (this is also possible from squares 1 and 3, but being corner squares they have already been eliminated). Only one square remains, the middle square at 5. You now confront your captor with your new discovery, made without having to move, and reveal your allegedly undiscoverable position.

Is this a genuine paradox? If not, why not? Where does the reasoning go wrong?

judiciously, to say: "You will hang at noon one day next week, but you will not be told which." In the above pseudo-paradoxes, the judge and the teacher go beyond this to make claims about the future expectations of the condemned man and the students, which goes beyond not only their jurisdiction, but the knowable truth. Judges have the power to hang, and to determine the moment of the hanging; but their authority does not entitle them to declare that a person shall be surprised. The prisoner, therefore, is not wise to assume that he must be surprised, or that if he is not then no hanging will take place.

SOLUTION

This pseudo-paradox is discussed by Sorensen (1982). As Sainsbury (1988) indicates, the appearance of paradox turns on the equivocation of a position being 1) discoverable by some set of two moves and 2) discoverable by any set of two moves. Many locations are discoverable by certain sets of two moves, but not by any sets of two moves. For example, the corner locations so crucial to the flawed logic above would not be revealed if you moved away from the wall rather than toward it.

When Reference Goes Wrong

Talking about stuff is something we do every day. We refer to things and make statements about them. If it were not so everyday an activity, it might appear more like the marvel it truly is. When it operates well it is innocuous and may be taken for granted; but at the boundaries, sometimes when pushed there deliberately, reference can go wrong.

Reference is the capacity we have to denote objects. Reference is also the relationship between words and what they stand for. The most straightforward cases are proper names (for example, "Socrates"), but general nouns (like "sand" or "panther") also denote types or pluralities of things. We also refer to completely ad hoc categories such as "things you might take camping." Also, to the extent that unvoiced thoughts still use words, reference is also achieved by ideas and thoughts. Even gestures such as pointing, a toss of the head, or a raised eyebrow refer to things. Meanwhile, quantification (words such as "some," "all," and "any") is a distinct but related phenomenon that enables our thoughts and language to take things into account, to be about the world, its contents, or ways it might be.

Meaning and Use

As individuals we discover a language in which words have their references intact. At a young age we learn that "duck" refers to those quacking birds that swim. However, from the wider perspective of humankind words are not discovered, but invented and introduced with a particular meaning. These meanings evolve and such changes are often introduced as novelties

before going on to become standardized. Words have the meanings they do because of social choices, but social choices are usually a *fait accompli* from the perspective of the individual, requiring rather than requesting his or her assent.

Of course, like Humpty Dumpty in *Alice's Adventures in Wonderland*, we all have the power to use words to refer randomly to whatever we might like. However, if we proceed to use our words to refer to anything we wish then it is impossible for us to communicate a coherent view of the world to one another. In fact, if words can mean anything we want them to, then one might just as well conclude that: 30[8sf d#fk?q \jao!e fP*-4mg}p vk%9o. And you can quote me on that!

Failures of Reference

Words can also fail to refer in other, perhaps more interesting ways. For example, "Pegasus" fails as there are no flying horses—Pegasus does not exist. Yet it seems true to say that Pegasus is a flying horse. Perhaps we could call this a "fictional truth," since, however true it may be, it does not entail that there exists at least one flying horse. (Contrast with this the valid argument that since Seabiscuit was a racehorse there was at least one racehorse.) Willard Van Orman Quine, an American logician, thought that instead of saying "Pegasus does not exist," one could say that nothing "pegasizes."

It is worth noting that another sort of failure of reference happens with definite descriptions—take the following example.

(i) The present king of Nepal is not wealthy. A problem arises here because there is no longer a king of Nepal, so the subject of the sentence fails to refer. If we therefore take statement **i** to be untrue, then its negation in the following statement ought to be true.

(ii) The present king of Nepal is wealthy. Again, however, we know this is not the case; and in order to prevent this conclusion, Bertrand Russell ingeniously analyzed sentences such as statement **i** along the following lines:

There is a present king of Nepal, and only one, and that person is not wealthy.

On account of its explicit logical structure, it is possible that this sentence can be false in different ways (for example, due to the end of the monarchy) that do not imply the wealth of the non-existent Nepalese crown.

That to Which You Cannot Refer
On close inspection, the situation depicted on this page becomes logically troubling. It might seem obvious that one could divide all reality into what we can refer to and everything else. The problem is that we can make no mention of everything else; because as soon as we do, we refer to it.

SEEING SIGNS
This sign refers to nothing. This is very different from not referring to anything, or not referring at all. Expressions that do not refer to anything are meaningless. This sign is not meaningless. It is not a failed sign.

NOTHING

Try explaining the diagram below to someone, without committing the logical sin of referring to what you cannot.

You cannot refer to what you cannot refer to. This statement not only seems true, it reads like a tautology, a redundant statement that only repeats in the predicate what is already explicit in the subject. But on a closer view, the subject itself is non-referring. If it refers at all, it will become self-contradictory. As a truth, it can't get off the ground.

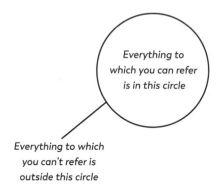

Everything to which you can refer is in this circle

Everything to which you can't refer is outside this circle

Self-Reference

It is sometimes said that reference is the capacity of words to stand for something beyond themselves. Though evocative, this is not very explanatory. Words may refer beyond themselves when we speak of the world, self, and others, but words can also stand for themselves. Words can self-refer. Many words are about words or ways of using them. But some words and combinations of words apply only to themselves.

The self-reference of words can be innocuous enough, so it is hard to maintain that there is something inherently suspect about it. For example, there are no obvious problems with either of the following sentences:

"This sentence is the first example in a list."

"This sentence is succinct."

Others, while perhaps more amusing, still present no problems for understanding:

"This sentence is self-referential."

"This speech will consist of a brief comment, followed by a few words of thanks. Thank you very much."

Inverted Self-Reference

One curiously indirect but common instance of self-reference occurs when people express their deepest feelings by saying: "Words cannot express how deeply I feel!"

It's an expression that everyone understands, so it is a very effective expression of deep feelings. However, the very sentence itself denies that it can communicate such deep emotions.

Other instances of self-reference are neither effective nor innocuous. Before we come to outright paradoxes arising from self-reference, let's look at another kind of problem that can occur—that of groundlessness. This occurs when self-reference keeps you spinning idly in circles, never able to track down the actual referent, like a dog chasing its own tail. It may be diverting, but it does not get you very far, and can quickly become annoying. Here is a well-scrutinized example:

(i) This sentence is true.
That sentence refers to itself. So does the following sentence, which is an accurate translation of statement **i** into French:

(ii) Cette phrase est vraie.
Do both sentences say the same thing? You'd think so, since they are correct translations of one another. Moreover, statement **i** says of itself what statement **ii** says of itself. And yet statements **i** and **ii** are not the same sentences; elles ne sont pas la même phrase. Two sentences referring to distinct sentences cannot possibly have the same meaning. So they cannot be asserting the same proposition. In a profound sense, they do not say the same thing.

But what does statement **i** mean? Philosophers account for the meanings of declarative sentences in different ways; for example, by specifying the conditions under which a sentence would be true; alternatively, by indicating what one would have to do in order to acquire evidence that it were true. For instance, it is quite clear what one would do to find out under what conditions a regular sentence like statement **iii** is true:

(iii) The new baby is a boy.
Statement **iii** makes a straightforward factual claim. Its conditions of truth are also straightforward. If the new baby is a boy, it is true; otherwise it is false. The underlying theory of truth here assumes that statement **iii** is true only if it corresponds to the facts. Alternatively, the meaning of such a sentence is indicated by the procedures of verification needed to determine its truth-value—here it is a case of simple observation, but elsewhere it could be counting, calculating, measuring, and so on.

However, applying either notion of meaning to statement **i** is problematic. To find out whether it is true, we should check if it corresponds to reality. That depends on whether the sentence it refers to is true, but that is what we need to find out. So round we go again, and rather frustratingly there is nothing we can do to get any closer to an answer. Similarly, thanks to self-reference, the reality that statement **i** refers to is itself; so it cannot be checked, except by being checked against itself. Once more we circle again and again back to the sentence itself, and it is therefore impossible to determine the truth or otherwise of statement **i**.

Based on either theory of meaning, the meaning of statement **i** is indeterminate; its proposition is all but empty. In its steadfast refusal to refer to anything beyond itself this sentence leaves us empty-handed, with nowhere to turn to observe anything that might verify it.

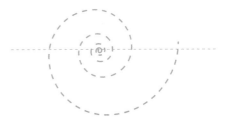

CHASING TRUTH

Imagine people standing in a circle, each pointing at the person to their right. One says: "What this person is about to say is true." You look to the person being pointed at to hear what they have to say, but they, also pointing at the person to the right of them, only say: "What this person is about to say is true." The next person does likewise, and you follow the chain around. You hope to receive some ultimate content, so you may finally verify the first claim, but at each turn you are again referred to someone else, until you find yourself back with the first person, who restates what he said earlier.

Can we say that the first statement is meaningless, when we understand what is said at each turn? Can all the parts be meaningful but the whole without meaning?

Self-Membership

As we have seen, some sentences are ungrounded—the example of this given on the previous page being: "This sentence is true." Any attempted verification cycles endlessly and never terminates. It overlaps with the reality it represents, and the correspondence is too close to be complete. Each time you try to establish the truth, any foundations upon which it could be based give way.

Introducing Sets

A related phenomenon exists in set-theory, known as "non-well-founded sets." Sets are simply collections of objects, and these objects are called "elements" or "members." Sets are identified by the members they have, so no two sets have exactly the same collection of members. A certain rule called the "Axiom of Foundation" ensures that sets are well-founded; that is, it prohibits sets from being members of themselves, or from being members of members of themselves, and so on. This axiom, however, is optional, almost ceremonial. Set theory without the axiom of foundation is logically consistent, provided set theory with the axiom is. Non-well-founded sets have been explored for a variety of applications.

Consider a set s with a single member, s itself. We can write $s \in s$—which is shorthand for "s is an element of s"; and also $s=\{s\}$— meaning "s is the singleton set containing only s as its member." This gives us an unending chain where s is an element of s, is an element of s, is an element of s, is an element of s ... This can be alternatively written as ... $s \in s \in s \in s \in s \in s$ ...

Look familiar? This non-well-founded set s is a lot like the ungrounded sentence: "This sentence is true." To identify s look to its member. However, s is its only member. One can keep unwrapping s but never reveal anything apart from the same old s hiding within it, waiting to be unwrapped.

Now consider set v, which is distinct from s as v is the singleton set containing only v as its member; or, to put it another way, $v=\{v\}$. The same reasoning as above also gives ... $v \in v \in v \in v \in v \in v$ ...

The set v is different from the set s, but they share the property of self-membership, of being their own singleton. You cannot get inside either of them, but you know that sets can only be distinguished by looking at their members. The ultimate grounds for their difference eternally evades us. (This is comparable to the way in which "This sentence is true" is distinct from "Cette phrase est vraie.")

Before we leave non-well-founded sets, consider now sets a and b (where a differs from b) such that $a=\{b\}$ and $b=\{a\}$. In this case a is a singleton, a set with one member, which is b. In turn b is also a set with a single member, namely a. So we have the curious infinite truth: ... $a \in b \in a \in b \in a \in b \in a \in b \in a$ ... We unpack one

box to find another, which we unpack in turn to find the first again.

This non-well-founded relationship bears a striking resemblance to the relation implied in the yin–yang symbol, where yin (dark) both surrounds and is in the center of yang (light), which both surrounds and is in the center of yin.

Non-Self-Membership

Groucho Marx famously said: "I don't care to belong to any club that will have me as a member." A witty aside for sure, but also a fine segue to Bertrand Russell's paradox of the set of all sets that do not contain themselves as elements (or members).

Before Russell, logicians had widely considered that one could form a set out of every collection of objects. For example, for any property or attribute, P, one could create a set of all the objects, x, with the attribute P—this set would be written as $\{x:Px\}$.

However, Russell showed this principle, called the Axiom of Comprehension, to be false. Ingeniously, he gave his objects the attribute: "is not a member of itself." That is, he let Px be $x \notin x$. In this case there should be a set $\{x:x \notin x\}$ that contains all of the sets that are not members of

themselves—a practical example of this might be an encyclopedia that lists every encyclopedia that does not contain an entry that refers to itself.

So far, so good. But what about the set itself? What are its properties? Should we list it with all of the other objects that boast the attribute "is not a member of itself"? Should our encyclopedia of encyclopedias contain a mention of its own existence?

Well, at first sight it appears it should not. To include such a self-referential entry in our encyclopedia would be breaking the condition that it "is not a member of itself." So let's leave any reference to itself out. Fine, the condition is now satisfied … or so it seems.

Now our encyclopedia doesn't mention itself, and this is where the paradox becomes apparent. By omitting to mention itself it now qualifies for the condition "is not a member of itself." Therefore, like the other encyclopedias that do not refer to themselves, it should surely be listed. But, as we've already seen, including it would break the condition that it "is not a member of itself."

Russell's paradox helped move set theory forward; however, our would-be compiler of the encyclopedia can go nowhere. For the encyclopedia to refer to itself means that it should not, but not to refer to itself means that it should. To the encyclopedia's poor editor this is an insoluble paradox—the only escape from which is most likely madness.

An I For a Me

We have already referred to, reference is something we do, and something that our words do. Words and sentences (including this one) can talk about themselves. This can result in paradox, but it often passes off innocently enough. However, when it comes to self-reference in the personal sense, a wealth of other conundrums and mysteries surface.

Speaking of Me...

We all know people who lack the social grace to speak about anything other than themselves. Personal self-reference can be as much a social *faux pas* as ungrounded claims like "This sentence is true" are logical *faux pas*. In the latter, no true step is taken; in the former, the step is real, but we only succeed in putting our foot in our mouth.

That we can refer to ourselves is an important part of our sense of self, and the sense that we are the same self, regardless of changes. All my experiences are irrevocably mine, which seems to imply that they all bear some reference to me as the subject and first-person witness of them all. And when I awake in the morning, I refer to the self who went to sleep the night before as myself, as this one, just now awoken.

Self-Reflection

Descartes's famous first principle, "I think, therefore I am," draws a metaphysical rabbit out of the hat of experience. Our experience invites self-reference; our existence legitimates it. Are you an event or an entity? Are you a who or a what?

Stigler's Law of Eponymy

Credit rarely settles where credit is due. History often lionizes a prominent but secondary mind, while real inventors are forgotten. Laws and discoveries are frequently attributed not to those upon whom they first dawned, but to lesser, more famous thinkers. So pervasive is this tendency that it has been formulated as Stigler's Law of Eponymy, according to which no scientific discovery is named for its original discoverer. Stephen Stigler named the law after himself, but had the insight to attribute it to someone else.

I Am Me

There can be very little doubt that, for anyone who utters it, the sentence "I am me" will express a truth. It is all too easy to discount this statement as an empty tautology, as void of content as the vacuous A=A. Surely, no one would disagree with either statement. (Well, almost no one! The great German philosopher Georg Hegel concluded in his *Science of Logic* that: "A is not A" and that "in itself then identity is absolute non-identity.") However, me, myself, and I know that there is a difference between these two identities. A=A is never informative, but in some cases "I am me" can be a revelation.

It happened to me, shortly after my fourth birthday. I was sitting alone on an old upholstered armchair, from the worn-out arms of which white balls of stuffing were extruding. My older siblings had sometimes attempted to alarm my younger siblings by pretending to eat this stuffing. They would remove the central portion of sliced white bread from the crust, roll it into a ball, and, with taunting mien, pop it into their mouths, thereby seeming to eat the furniture. Being a middle child, I saw through the jest. But that day I happened to be all alone eating bread, and I had rolled up the white part into a ball. Taunting myself that I was eating the stuffing, I bit into my round white morsel and was very surprised to discover that it was…bread! I had succeeded in fooling myself, and had now been exposed to myself. It was then that I experienced my first existential moment. The insight came to me as a remarkable surprise: I am me.

Only years later did I learn of the famous distinction drawn by the American psychologist and philosopher William James between I, the subject of my experience, and me, the object of my experience. I am the witness to my experience—the I is myself as the subject of my subjectivity. But I also experience myself as an object—for instance, when I pat my body and say, *this is me*, as if to remind myself of my corporeal existence. This object, this me, is also available to other subjects, other people in my environment, such as parents and siblings. The me is physical and social, the me is shared publicly; however, the I is personal and mental, the I remains private.

To play a joke on myself successfully, I had to separate subject and object, I and me. I had to think one thing, and think that "me" was thinking something else. When I fooled myself, I realized I was right: the "me" had been taken in, and was in error.

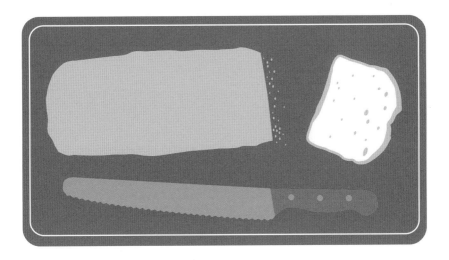

The Liar Paradox

The so-called Liar Paradox has biblical authority, in St. Paul's letter to Titus: "Even one of their own prophets has said, 'Cretans are always liars, evil brutes, lazy gluttons.' This testimony is true." (Titus 1:12–13)

If, as Paul says, the testimony is true, then Cretans are always liars. If always to be a liar is always to lie, then this testimony is a lie. Paul ought not to have claimed it was true. If, contrary to Paul, the testimony is not true, then Cretans are not always liars, which means sometimes they are not liars. For instance, some of them may have reformed and sworn off lying, possibly even this particular prophet. What he says is untrue, but he may be guilty of hyperbole rather than any intent to deceive. But for Paul's vouching for the testimony, it is not inconsistent to call it false. In context, it seems more likely that the saint is making a joke, rather than an earnest logical critique.

How Not to Lie

Despite its misformulation in the Bible, the Liar Paradox has nothing to do with lies. Liars are types of persons; to be always a liar is always to be that sort of person. But that sort of person does not necessarily always lie. To be a genuine liar, it is enough if one regularly or routinely lies, so one cannot be counted on to tell the truth. Moreover, to lie is to intend to deceive. So although "I am now lying" might be mistaken for a version of the Liar Paradox, it is merely a failed speech act.

Now, this sort of forthright disclosure is not the *modus operandi* of most liars, who generally need to hide the fact that they are lying in order to make themselves plausible.

A liar must tell many truths to pull off one believable lie. To openly confess to be lying while in the act is simply to give oneself away, and deceive no one. Anyone who tells you they are lying to you is not deceiving you, and is at most attempting to lie, and doing a very poor job of it. They say they are lying, and they are certainly speaking falsely; but though what they say is untrue, their intention to deceive is abandoned in the confession.

A More Believable Liar

The best forms of the Liar Paradox don't mention lying at all. They simply mention truth or its lack. The following mention only falsity:

(i) "What I am now stating is false."
(ii) "This sentence is false."
(iii) "The proposition expressed by the previous sentence is false."
(iv) "The proposition expressed by the present sentence is false."

Statement **i** and especially **ii** are the most direct forms. Statement **iii** introduces the important but controversial notion of the proposition. When a sentence is used to claim a truth, that claim is called a proposition. You can say the same thing in different ways, using different words—while the proposition remains the same. Radically different sentences (for example, from different languages) might express the same proposition. Propositions are abstract objects that some philosophers regard as the primary bearers of the values "true" or "false." Sentences, even thoughts and beliefs, are then considered true or false only in so far as they represent a proposition which is true or false. Statement **iv** locates the paradox in the proposition, not merely in the sentence used to express it.

The Law of Bivalence

Try reasoning through the arguments showing each of **i** to **iv** to be genuine paradoxes. (Start by assuming each is true and prove this is not true; then assume each is false and prove this is not true.)

If you are attentive, you will notice that your arguments depend upon the Law of Bivalence, which states that every proposition is either true or false. (An interesting contrast to the degrees of truth examined on p. 55.)

Questioning bivalence means that we must allow for truth-values somewhere between the absolutes "true" and "false." Half-truths, degrees of truth, or various third values have been proposed. Perhaps, besides true and false, there is another truth-value, let's call it "quizzical." In this light, sentence **ii** is not false, as it claims, but quizzical, from which it decidedly does not follow that it is true. In this way, our paradox is averted.

A QUIZZICAL SENTENCE

A third truth value, such as quizzical, may avert one paradox, but gets into another that is just as bad. Consider the following: "This sentence is either quizzical or false." Assuming all three truth values, show that contradiction arises even without bivalence.

Hint: A disjunction is quizzical if at least one of its disjuncts is quizzical.

Paradoxes arise even without assuming bivalence. This can be seen in another

way, by substituting "not true" for "false" throughout our examples. If you reason through the amended versions, you will notice that a different underlying logical principle is required. Known as the Law of Excluded Middle, it states that every proposition is either true or not true. In practice, both bivalence and the excluded middle are difficult laws to dispense with, but it has not been beyond the ingenuity of philosophers to try.

SOLUTION

"This sentence is either quizzical or false" is true! If true, this sentence is either quizzical or false. In either case it is not true. If false, the sentence is neither quizzical nor false. So it is not false. Since it is neither true nor false, it must be quizzical. But if quizzical, then the first of its disjuncts is true. But that entails that

From Ridiculous Paradoxes to Sublime Truths

While some of the paradoxes we have considered offer little more than amusement value, others reach into the depths of all things logical. Here we see that in some cases there is only the thinnest of lines between whimsical paradox and profound theorem.

We saw that the Liar Paradox is not really about lying. It can be formulated without mention of lying or the implication of the intent to deceive. All that is needed is the notion of falsity, and even that can be replaced by truth and negation. It turns out, however, that neither falsity nor negation are necessary concepts: a comparable paradox can arise without either, relying solely on the notion of truth and the power of self-reference.

Here we go: Let A be any sentence. Then let B be the following sentence.

(B) If B is true, so is A.

Clearly, if B is true then the antecedent (or "if-clause") of B is true (since B is its own antecedent). But if the conditional B is true, and its antecedent is true, then its consequent (or "then-clause") must also be true. A is the consequent of B, and therefore A must be true.

This sounds reasonable, except that A is any sentence at all. We have just proven absolutely anything. Moreover we have used no negations at all in doing so, showing that the so-called Liar Paradox can arise from a combination of truth and self-reference alone.

The Unprovable Liar

An interesting thing happens in these self-referential paradoxes if we replace the idea of truth with the idea of proof. Instead of finding a contradiction, one unveils major theorems of logic, specifically Kurt Gödel's incompleteness theorems. Let's start with another specious paradox, and see where it goes wrong.

"What I am saying cannot be proved."

Suppose this statement can be proved. Then what it says must be true. But it says it cannot be proved. If we assume it can be proved, we prove it cannot be proved. So our supposition that it was provable is wrong. With that road closed to us, let's try the only other one available—let's suppose it cannot be proved. Since that is precisely what it says, then it is true after all. And this ends our proof of the above statement!

The Problem

This paradox is not genuine. It depends upon an ambiguity of the word "proof." In everyday use, proof simply means good, strong evidence. Anything you can show to be true is proved. However, in mathematics, proof is defined more precisely. A proof is a finite sequence of well-formed formulas (for example, in the language of arithmetic) such that each one is either an instance of an axiom or follows from previous formulas in the list in accordance with certain rules of inference.

These rules are defined formally so as to lead only from one truth to the next. The set of provable formulas is always defined relative to a formal language, a set of axioms expressed in that same language, and a set of permissible rules. If you stick to a precise notion of provability in a particular logical system, then the arguments for apparent paradoxes discussed above can be seen to be fallacious.

From Paradox to Theorem

Instead of a genuine paradox, a remarkable fact about mathematics is unveiled—that it is incomplete.

A precise notion of provability allows one to separate the concept of provability from the concept of truth. The set of truths of arithmetic, for example, is not necessarily the same as the set of theorems provable in a given axiomatization of arithmetic. Indeed, they are not the same. In short, no system of arithmetic can prove every mathematical truth.

Gödel was able to construct, for every system of arithmetic, an arithmetical

formula that was true but unprovable in that system. You could know it was true, but you would also know that it was unprovable in your system. It may well be provable in a different system (starting, say, from a different set of axioms); but that system too would have a hole in it, and would itself leave out some truths of arithmetic.

So, how did Gödel prove this incompleteness? Cleverly, he found a simple way to express a formula in each system that asserted its own unprovability within that system. It asserted: "I am unprovable."

Gödel was able to do this by treating proofs as statements of arithmetic. He assigned all formulas unique numbers, and then also all sequences of formulas. With this coding, he could always find the number of a formula that said in effect: "This statement is not provable in this system."

If it was provable within the particular system, then the formula was untrue—it did, after all, claim to be unprovable. In this case, the system itself is in trouble as it has just proven a false statement.

If, however, the formula is unprovable in that system, then it is true. You can know the formula but it cannot be proven. The system is incomplete.

Exercise 3

Yablo's Paradox

THE PROBLEM:

"Many are called, few are chosen." In other words, there is always an infinite lineup to get into heaven, but not everyone qualifies for entry. Each one in line wonders if they will be that last one, and whether or not others in the line with them are honest and have truthful thoughts. Let us suppose that, at a certain moment, everyone in the line has a thought which each can express with the following words: "What all those behind me in line are thinking at this instant is untrue." Show that the thought each person in line is thinking at the given moment is paradoxical, both true and false.

THE METHOD:

This paradox is adapted from one developed by Roy Sorensen, which was itself modeled on a paradox original to Stephen Yablo. Here we discuss Yablo's Paradox as a way to suggest to the reader a solution to the infinite lineup problem.

Yablo's Paradox consists of an infinitely long list of sentences which cannot be assigned truth-values (true or false) in a logically consistent manner:

(1) All of the following sentences are untrue.

(2) All of the following sentences are untrue.

(3) All of the following sentences are untrue.

(4) All of the following sentences are untrue.

To see the problem, one can show that the first sentence can be neither true nor false. That is, we seek to derive a contradiction from the assumption that (1) is true. That will show (1) must be false, but again we can derive a contradiction from the assumption that (1) is false, as well.

If (1) is true, then all the rest are untrue—for that is just what (1) says. But if all the rest of the sentences are untrue, then so are all the sentences following (2) (a subset of all those coming after (1)). In that case, clearly, sentences (3) and onward are untrue. Now this is exactly what (2) says, so (2) is true after all. So if (1) is true, (2) is both true and untrue. That is impossible, so (1) must be untrue.

Now if, as this suggests, we assume on the contrary that (1) is untrue, then not all of the sentences that follow it can be untrue. In other words, at least one of the sentences after (1) must be true. Call that sentence (k). (k) is true, so every sentence after (k) will be untrue (including sentence k+1); after all, that is just what sentence (k) says. Trivially, every sentence after k+1 will therefore be untrue. This, however, is just what sentence k+1 says! So sentence k+1 is true, even though we just saw that it is untrue (it comes after sentence (k), which is true). Thus, if sentence (1) is untrue, the contradiction is merely postponed, put off till later. Sentence (1) can't be true, but it can't be false either. Thus the paradox.

Notice that, if (1) is true, all those after it are untrue (since that is what sentence (1) says). Notice too that what makes any given sentence in the list true is already included in what makes sentence (1) true, since later sentences always refer to a subset of the list sentence (1) refers to. As a consequence, if sentence (1) is true, all the rest are true. Consequently, if (1) is true, all the sentences after it are paradoxical, both true and untrue. So (1) must not be true; but then, as we have just seen, the contradiction is merely postponed. At least one of the later sentences must be true, and then everyone after it will be paradoxical.

THE SOLUTION:

The Yablo paradox is an infinite variation on the simple liar paradox (see p. 72). Unlike other liar-type paradoxes, it does not seem to involve self-reference (see p. 66),

although this claim has been disputed (for instance, does anyone in the line refer to their own thoughts?). The issue has been considered important, because the elimination of self-reference has been sometimes proposed (by self-appointed paradox-police) as a solution to all the paradoxes. Such a solution would present problems for this book, not just because p. 66 and the current page refer to each other, which the censors of self-reference would not allow, but also because the very subject of the present book (which it is self-referential to mention) would be obliterated.

Such threats to the very existence of this book need not detain us from mentioning that the lineup puzzle can be seen to be paradoxical as follows. Suppose that someone in line is thinking a true thought at the crucial instant of interest. Call that person k. Since k's thought is true, then everyone after k would have an untrue thought. (k would thus be the last in line to get into heaven, since those with untrue thoughts are disqualified.) But if the thoughts on everyone's mind who is after k are untrue, then clearly thoughts on everyone's mind who is after k+1 are untrue. This makes the thought on the mind of k+1 both untrue (because k+1 comes after k, and all those after k in line have untrue thoughts) and paradoxically also true (for it merely says that a simple subset of the above have untrue thoughts).

It follows that k's thought at the moment in question is not, after all, true. So at least one person j>k has a true thought at that very instant. It will follow, by exactly similar reasoning, that the thought on the mind of j+1 will be both untrue and true.

Chapter 4

Mathematical Paradoxes

Numbers and infinity are the home of many paradoxes, both apparent and genuine, amusing and mind-blowing. Before examining a few illusory paradoxes, we look at deeper puzzles that are only resolved in a mathematical theory of infinity. Infinities are strange, in that they are the same size as proper parts of themselves, and because there are infinities upon infinities, so that for every infinite size there is a larger infinite size. Clearly there is more to infinity than merely everything.

Spoof Proofs

The following paradox is usually credited to the British mathematician and logician Augustus De Morgan (1806–1871), and is a real humdinger. Using elementary algebra, De Morgan proves that if $x = 1$ then $x = 0$: a conclusion so patently absurd that there simply must be an error. But where? Here's De Morgan's proof...

Step 1: $x = 1$

Step 2: Multiply both sides by x
$$x^2 = x$$

Step 3: Subtract 1 from each side
$$x^2 - 1 = x - 1$$

Step 4: Divide both sides by $x-1$
$$\frac{x^2-1}{x-1} = \frac{x-1}{x-1}$$

Now, from high-school algebra you may remember that $x^2 - 1 = (x+1)(x-1)$. If you've forgotten this, just search for the phrase "difference of two squares" online for a reminder. So, to continue...

Step 5: $\dfrac{(x+1)(x-1)}{x-1} = \dfrac{x-1}{x-1}$

Step 6: Cancel out the factor $(x-1)$
$$\frac{(x+1)\cancel{(x-1)}}{\cancel{x-1}} = \frac{\cancel{x-1}}{\cancel{x-1}}$$

Step 7: Thus
$$x+1 = 1$$

Step 8: Subtract 1 from both sides
$$x = 0$$

Beautiful! A clear demonstration that if $x = 1$ then $x = 0$, surely a perfect paradox if ever there was one.

In fact, this is not really a paradox at all, but rather a fallacy. A genuine paradox reaches its absurd, surprising, or contradictory conclusion by means of apparently valid reasoning. But in this case, the math contains a clear-cut, albeit difficult to spot, error. De Morgan was, of course, aware of this and offered his "proof" merely as a puzzle or curiosity.

Before reading on, why not see if you can spot the error for yourself?

A CHALLENGE...

Work through the following "proof" that 2 = 1. See if you can spot the error.

Step 1: Let a and b be equal and non-zero $a = b$

Step 2: Multiply both sides by a $a^2 = ab$

Step 3: Subtract b^2 $a^2 - b^2 = ab - b^2$

Step 4: Factorize $(a+b)(a-b) = b(a-b)$

Step 5: Divide by $(a-b)$ $a + b = b$

Step 6: But $a = b$ (initial assumption). So ... $b + b = b$

Step 7: Therefore $2b = b$

Step 8: Divide both sides by b $2 = 1$

SOLUTION

Once again, the error is in attempting to divide by zero, this time in line 5.

The Flaw in De Morgan's "Proof"

The error occurs in step 4 where both sides are divided by $x-1$. This seems an innocuous enough step, until you remember that the proof begins with the premise, $x = 1$. So dividing by $x-1$ amounts to dividing by zero, which is a mathematical no-no.

To understand why division by zero is ruled out in mathematics we must go back to the definition of division. It is defined as the inverse of multiplication. In other words, $a \div b = c$ means the same as $c \times b = a$. Or, using a concrete example, $8 \div 4 = 2$ means $2 \times 4 = 8$.

Attempting to divide by zero leads to all kinds of trouble. By definition, $a \div b = c$ means $c \times b = a$. But what happens when $b = 0$? In this case, we have, $a \div 0 = c$, which means $c \times 0 = a$. But this makes no sense. If a is non-zero then there is no value of c such that $c \times 0 = a$; and if a is equal to zero then any value of c will suffice.

Division by zero makes no sense and is therefore ruled out in mathematics. Thus step 4 in De Morgan's proof is illegal, and everything that follows is meaningless.

The Missing Dollar Riddle

Purists will be scandalized to find a mere riddle in this book of paradoxes. But the Missing Dollar Riddle does fit the, admittedly rather loose, definition of a paradox given in the Introduction: an absurd, contradictory, or counterintuitive conclusion derived from apparently valid reasoning. In any case, the Missing Dollar Riddle is far too much fun to leave out.

Three people have dinner at a restaurant. After the meal, the waiter brings over the bill, which comes to $30. So each diner contributes $10.

The waiter takes the cash to the manager, who informs him that a mistake was made adding up the bill. The actual cost of the meal was just $25. So the diners have been overcharged $5.

The manager hands five $1 bills to the waiter and tells him to return them to the diners. However, the waiter is not entirely honest. Rather than handing over all five $1 bills, he hands over just three of them. He gives one to each diner, and keeps two for himself.

But there is something amiss here. The three diners end up paying $9 each, making a total of $27. Meanwhile, the waiter pockets $2. But $27 plus $2 adds up to just $29 rather than the original $30. Where is the missing dollar?

A Classic Conundrum

The Missing Dollar Riddle is a classic brainteaser: a perennial puzzle that resurfaces every so often to flummox and befuddle a new generation of victims. In 2003 it formed the basis of an e-mail chain-letter, which contained the bogus promise, "Send this to five people and the answer will appear on your screen."

ANOTHER PUZZLE

Here's another missing-dollar type puzzle. See if you can solve it.

A man sells apples at a local market: three large apples for a dollar, or five small ones for a dollar. At lunchtime, the man leaves his daughter in charge of the stall. Before he goes, he counts the remaining apples. There are 30 big ones and 30 small ones.

When the man returns, his daughter announces that she has sold all of the remaining apples—and hands over $15.

"That's not right," the man protests. "Thirty big apples at three for a dollar comes to $10; and thirty small apples at five for a dollar comes to $6. There should be $16."

"But that's all the money I took," the girl insists. "And I did my calculations carefully. A lady came along who wanted to buy all the apples. So rather than worrying about which were large and which were small, I charged her the average price of four for a dollar. There are fifteen fours in sixty. So that's a total of $15."

What happened to the missing dollar?

SOLUTION

The girl assumed that she could charge the "average price" of four for a dollar for the apples. That's 25¢ apiece. In fact, the average price per apple works out at a little under 27¢. The father correctly calculated that the total cost for all the apples is $16. Divide that by 60 and you get 26.6¢ per fruit. An "average" group of four apples consists of two big ones and two small ones. Big ones cost 33.3¢ ($1÷3) and small ones 20¢ ($1÷5). So rather than four for a dollar, she should have charged four for for $1.06!

The appeal of the puzzle lies in its quasi-paradoxical nature. A very simple story, combined with some elementary arithmetic, leads to a baffling conclusion. Even when the solution is offered, many people still don't feel entirely happy—and continue to fret over the missing dollar.

The Missing Dollar Revealed

The Missing Dollar Riddle is a scam. A cunning and really rather beautiful scam. But a scam nonetheless.

The riddle invites us to add the $27 paid by the diners to the $2 in the waiter's pocket, and then to marvel that the total comes to only $29. But there is no logical reason to add those two amounts. The $2 in the waiter's pocket is part of the $27 paid by the diners.

Look at it this way. Between them, the three diners paid $27. Twenty-five of those dollars went into the restaurant's cash-box, and the other two went into the waiter's pocket. No problem.

Or look at it this way. The three diners handed over $30 to the waiter. $25 went into the cash-box; the waiter kept $2 for himself; and the diners received a $3 refund. $25 + $2 + $3 = $30. Again, no problem.

In short, there is no missing dollar.

Reductio Ad Absurdum

Sometimes, in mathematics, an apparent paradox arises because of faulty reasoning (see pp. 80–81). Once the error has been identified, the paradox simply melts away. But what happens when no error can be found? Surprisingly, this can be a very good thing indeed...

How Many Prime Numbers?

A prime number is a natural number that has only two factors: 1 and itself. So 7 is prime because it only has factors 1 and 7, whereas 9 is non-prime since it has the factors 1, 3, and 9. The first 10 prime numbers are: 2, 3, 5, 7, 11, 13, 17, 19, 23, and 29.

Non-primes can always be broken down into prime factors (for example, 30 = 2 x 3 x 5). Prime numbers, of course, cannot.

How many prime numbers are there? Does the list go on forever? Or is there a very last prime? On the face of it, these questions seem unanswerable. After all, we cannot possibly test all of the natural numbers to see if they are prime, since there are infinitely many of them.

Euclid Investigates

However, when the Greek mathematician Euclid applied himself to this problem some 2,300 years ago, he managed to come up with a definitive answer. His reasoning went like this.

Let us assume that there is a finite number of primes, the largest being p. Thus, the complete list of primes runs:

2, 3, 5, 7, 11, 13 ... p

Now, let us multiply all of these prime numbers together to get a product, which we will call n:

2 x 3 x 5 x 7 x 11 x 13 x ... x p = n

So far so good. Note that every prime number is therefore a factor of n.

Now consider the number $n+1$. Clearly, if we divide this by any prime number we will be left with a remainder of 1. So $n+1$ has no prime factors.

But any number that has no prime factors is, by definition, a prime number. So either $n+1$ is prime, or it has prime factors greater than p that we haven't accounted for. Either way, p is not the largest prime.

But this is absurd. We have a paradox. We began by assuming that there is a largest prime, p, and proceeded to prove that p is not the largest prime!

Reductio Ad Absurdum

Given the contradiction arising from Euclid's analysis, our first thought might be to check for errors in his reasoning. If an error can be found, then the apparent paradox can be downgraded to a mere fallacy. This is precisely what happened in the case of De Morgan's spoof proof that if $x = 1$ then $x = 0$.

But in this case, there are no errors. Euclid's reasoning is impeccable. We have a situation where the assumption that there is a largest prime leads inexorably to the conclusion that there must be a still larger one.

Since the initial assumption leads logically to an absurdity, we must conclude that the assumption itself is incorrect. It is simply wrong to assume that there is a largest prime number. Knowing this, we can confidently assert that there is no largest prime number. Instead, there are infinitely many of them.

This type of argument, where a proposition is proved by showing that its opposite leads to a contradiction, is known as "reductio ad absurdum" (Latin, meaning "reduction to absurdity").

This subtle and indirect method of proof is much beloved of mathematicians and philosophers; in fact, the English mathematician G. H. Hardy described it as "one of a mathematician's finest weapons."

Some Paradoxes of Infinity

The following paradox derives from Albert of Saxony (1316–1390), a medieval philosopher and logician.

A Paradox Concerning Cubes

Imagine taking an infinitely long plank of wood, with a square cross-section, and slicing it up into cubes. How many cubes could we make? An infinite number of cubes, obviously.

Now imagine taking one of those cubes and surrounding it with some of its companions to make a larger one (something like a Rubik's Cube). This would require a total of 3 x 3 x 3 = 27 small cubes. We could then surround our 3 x 3 x 3 cube to make a 5 x 5 x 5 one. This would require an additional 98 (53–33) small cubes.

We could keep going like this forever. It would require an additional 218 small cubes to turn our 5 x 5 x 5 cube into a 7 x 7 x 7; and yet another 386 to increase it to a 9 x 9 x 9; and so on.

The number of small cubes required grows alarmingly, but this need not concern us since we have an infinite supply. In fact, our infinitely long plank can be used to construct a cube of infinite volume!

To gain an appreciation of just how mind-boggling this is, picture the original plank as a very slender one, say, just ½in by ½₂in in cross section, but stretching off to infinity. This slender beam could be used to make a cube that fills infinite three-dimensional space.

More Weirdness

The ninth-century Arab mathematician Thabit ibn Qurra pointed out that infinity can be split in half, and each half will remain infinite. For example, the infinite series of natural numbers (1, 2, 3, 4, 5, 6 …) can be split into odds (1, 3, 5, 7…) and evens (2, 4, 6, 8 …), both of which are infinite. So infinity minus infinity appears to be … infinity.

In 1638 the Italian scientist Galileo brought to light another perplexing feature of infinity. A line contains an infinite number of points. But clearly some lines are longer than others. Thus we appear to have something greater than infinity, because the infinity of points in the longer line is greater than the infinity of points in the shorter line.

Further proof (if any were needed) that infinity is a very strange beast can be found on the following pages.

SHUT UP

When my brother Stephen and I were children, we would often come into conflict with one another. Sometimes, in an attempt to resolve these fraternal disputes without recourse to violence, we would engage in rational discourse:

Stephen: Shut up!

Gary: Shut up, yourself!

Stephen: Double shut up!

Gary: Triple shut up!

Stephen: Shut up times a thousand!

Gary: Shut up times a million!

Stephen: Shut up, a million and one!

Gary: Shut up, to infinity!

Stephen: Shut up, to infinity plus one!

Gary (triumphantly): There's nothing bigger than infinity!

I always considered the last remark an outright clincher. But do you think I was correct? Read on to the end of the chapter to see if you change your mind.

Galileo's Paradox

This mind-boggling paradox about infinity was discovered by the Italian scientist Galileo Galilei (1564–1642). He published it in 1638 in his *Dialogues Concerning Two New Sciences.*

Natural and Square Numbers

Consider the list of natural (in other words positive whole) numbers: 1, 2, 3, 4, 5, 6, 7…

A moment's reflection should convince you that the list is infinite. No matter how high you count, you can always keep going.

Next consider the list of square numbers. You get a square number whenever you multiply another number by itself. For example, 1 is a square number because it is equal to 1 x 1; 4 is a square number because it is equal to 2 x 2; and so on. Thus the list of squares runs: 1, 4, 9, 16, 25, 36, 49…

Again, a moment's reflection should convince you that this list too is infinite. However high you go, there'll always be more squares.

So, which is bigger, the list of natural numbers or the list of squares? See if you can work it out before continuing.

Naturals versus Squares

The list of natural numbers contains both squares and non-squares, whereas the list of square numbers contains only squares. Thus, all of the square numbers are contained within the list of natural numbers. In mathematical terms, we say that the squares form a subset (technically, a proper subset) of the set of natural numbers. Clearly, therefore, there are more naturals than squares.

To illustrate this we can write the two lists one beneath the other:

Natural numbers:
1 2 3 4 5 6 7 8 9 10 11 12 13 14 15 16…

Squares:
1   4   9   16…

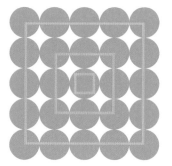

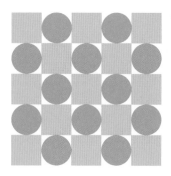

From which it is crystal clear that the naturals outnumber the squares. In fact, the squares become more and more sparse as the list of natural numbers grows.

But there is an alternative way of looking at this, which yields a very different result. Ask yourself precisely how many square numbers there are, and you will see that there is exactly one square corresponding to every natural number. This is because every natural number can be multiplied by itself to yield a square. Therefore, the number of squares is equal to the number of naturals.

To illustrate this, we can write the lists one beneath the other:

Natural numbers:
1 2 3 4 5 6 7 8 9 10 11…

Square numbers:
1 4 9 16 25 36 49 64 81 100 121…

Evidently, the lists are the same size.

Infinity Is a Very Strange Beast
This, then, is Galileo's Paradox. Careful reasoning reveals that the natural numbers outnumber the squares. But equally careful reasoning reveals that there are equal amounts of squares and naturals.

Galileo thought deeply about this, and concluded that the concept of infinity is beyond human understanding. More specifically, he claimed that attributes such as "equal to," "greater than," and "less than" cannot be meaningfully applied to infinite quantities, only to finite ones.

QUESTIONS OF INFINITY

1. How many even numbers are there?
2. How many odd numbers are there?
3. Which are more numerous, the natural numbers or the even numbers?
4. Which are more numerous, the even numbers or the odd?

GALILEO AND INFINITY
There is an infinite quantity of even numbers and an infinite quantity of odds. According to Galileo, questions 3 and 4 are meaningless since concepts like "greater than," "less than," and "equal to" cannot be applied to infinite quantities. But was Galileo right? Find out by reading on to the end of the chapter.

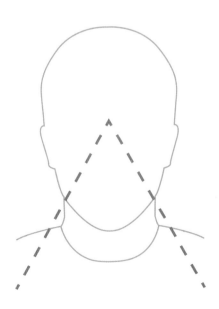

Finite and Infinite Sets

Galileo's insightful analysis of the natural and square numbers led to the paradox shown on the previous page. The list of natural numbers contains both squares and non-squares; and yet there appear to be no more natural numbers than squares.

This convinced Galileo that infinity is beyond human comprehension, and that attributes like "greater than," "less than," and "equal to" cannot be meaningfully applied to infinite quantities.

Galileo reasoned like this. The concept of infinity gives rise to mathematical paradoxes. Therefore infinity must be banished from our thinking. Trying to incorporate it into mathematics or anything else can only lead to disaster.

This was the prevailing opinion for the next two centuries or so. But then along came Georg Cantor, a German mathematician who was not content to dismiss the infinite, but sought instead to understand it.

Cantor succeeded in doing something that Galileo had considered impossible: he found a way to compare the sizes of infinite collections.

Sets and Their Sizes

Mathematicians sometimes talk about "sets," and we've already encountered these on pp. 68–69. To recap, for our purposes, we can think of a set simply as a collection of objects or elements, which can be real or mental. A set's *cardinality* is the number of elements it contains. For example, the cardinality of the set of vowels in the English alphabet, {a, e, i, o, u}, is 5. You can compare the cardinality or size

of two finite sets by simply counting the elements in each. For example, since there are five vowels compared to twenty-one consonants in the English alphabet, the set of consonants is larger.

But there is another, sometimes more convenient, way to compare the size of two sets. Suppose you want to compare the numbers of boys and girls in a school playground. The quickest way would be to pair off the pupils, boy/girl, boy/girl, boy/girl, and see if there are any pupils left over. If there are excess girls then clearly the set of girls is larger; whereas if there are excess boys then the set of boys is larger. If boys and girls pair off neatly then the two sets are the same size.

So, two finite sets are the same size if we can establish a one-to-one correspondence between their members. That is, if we can pair them off neatly, with no leftovers. So much for finite sets. But what about infinite ones?

Pairing Off Infinite Sets

Sometimes it is a straightforward matter to pair-off the elements of two infinite sets. Take the sets of odd and even numbers, for example:

Odds: 1 3 5 7 9 11 13 15 17...
Evens: 2 4 6 8 10 12 14 16 18...

Clearly the elements can be matched one to one. This makes perfect sense, since we feel intuitively that the two sets have the same cardinality.

But what about the natural and square numbers? Galileo demonstrated that they too can be paired off neatly if we go about it the right way:

Natural numbers: 1 2 3 4 5 6 7...
Square numbers: 1 4 9 16 25 36 49...

This suggests that the two sets are the same size, although intuitively we feel that there ought to be more naturals than squares.

In a similar way, the natural numbers can be matched one to one with the even numbers, despite the fact that intuitively we feel the natural numbers must be twice as numerous.

Natural numbers: 1 2 3 4 5 6 7...
Even numbers: 2 4 6 8 10 12 14...

It turns out that all infinite sets made from natural numbers (odds, evens, squares, cubes, and so on) can be matched one to one with one another. This suggests that all such infinite sets are the same size, which is a very counterintuitive, and indeed paradoxical result.

Just to make the paradox clear, consider once more the natural and the square numbers. One-to-one correspondence suggests that the two sets are the same size, and yet the square numbers are a mere subset of the naturals. How is this paradox to be avoided?

The obvious solution, à la Galileo, is to deny the existence of infinite sets and banish them from mathematics. But Cantor took the opposite tack. Instead of sidestepping the paradox, he embraced it.

Cantor defined an infinite set as one that can be put into a one-to-one correspondence with a subset of itself. This means that an infinite set has the mind-boggling property that its whole is no larger than some of its parts.

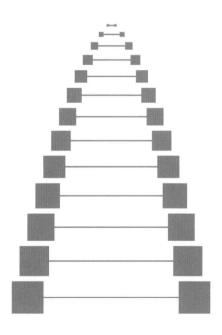

Profile

Georg Cantor

Up until the nineteenth century, most mathematicians tried to avoid paradoxes by steering clear of infinity. But not so the German mathematician Georg Cantor (1845–1918).

He possessed the genius and the audacity to embrace it. He treated infinity like any other mathematical quantity: as something you can manipulate, and work with, and build into theorems. In fact, he worked out a whole arithmetic of infinity.

To say that his ideas were controversial would be an understatement. Some "finitist" mathematicians took a very dim view of what he was trying to achieve, and opposed or ridiculed him. Chief among them was Leopold Kronecker, a former professor of Cantor's, and a very influential figure in the mathematical community of the time.

Kronecker was certain that all discussion of infinite sets was illegitimate, because infinite sets do not exist. "God created the natural numbers, and all the rest is the work of man," he once remarked.

Early in Cantor's career, Kronecker had given him encouragement and support. But once Cantor began working on the mathematics of infinity, Kronecker turned on him. Never one to mince his words, he called Cantor a "corruptor of youth" and dismissed his work as "humbug."

As a result of such opposition, Cantor suffered many personal and professional setbacks. He spent his entire career stuck in the mathematical backwater of Halle University and always struggled to achieve any great recognition.

Cantor was high strung, and therefore painfully sensitive to Kronecker's plotting and sniping. His mental health suffered accordingly. In 1884 he had a nervous breakdown, and from that time onward suffered intermittent bouts of mental illness. At times, he turned away from mathematical research altogether, and absorbed himself in history and theology instead.

Interestingly, his ideas about infinity gained more support from the theologians of the Catholic Church than from his fellow mathematicians. This was largely thanks to a priest named Constantin Gutberlet, who embraced the notion that the intellect could comprehend infinity, since this seemed to offer a way for human minds to penetrate more deeply into the divine nature.

Furthermore, the existence of actual, rather than merely potential, infinities amounted to a feather in the cap of the Almighty. Kronecker claimed that God had created only finite numbers. But if God were the creator of the infinite as well as the finite, it would resound more greatly to His glory.

Cantor became intensely interested in the theological implications of his work on infinity, and relished the opportunity to discuss his ideas with a sympathetic audience. He came to view his theorems as

instruments in the service of God and the Catholic Church.

Kronecker died in 1891. From that time on, opposition to Cantor's ideas began to peter out, and they started to become more and more widely accepted among mathematicians. In the latter part of his life he began to receive some of the recognition he deserved. But by then his mathematical powers had waned, and he continued to suffer periods of mental instability. He died in January 1918.

Today most, but not all, mathematicians accept his ideas. He is celebrated as one of history's great mathematicians: a pioneering genius who invented set theory, and provided the foundations for the mathematical understanding of infinite collections.

In 1926, another German mathematician, David Hilbert (see pp. 94–95), wrote, "No one will drive us from the paradise which Cantor created for us."

Hilbert's Hotel

The German mathematician David Hilbert (1863–1943) illustrated the paradoxical nature of the infinite using the striking example of a hotel—but a hotel very different to any that you or I have ever visited.

When an ordinary hotel with a finite number of rooms is full, it's full. There's no way to accommodate an extra guest without first evicting an existing one. But a hotel with an infinite number of rooms is different. It can always accommodate newcomers—even when it's full.

Consider Hilbert's Hotel. It has an infinite number of rooms, numbered 1, 2, 3, 4, 5… and so on. A prospective guest arrives, and is disappointed to learn that every room is occupied. "Don't worry," says the manager. "I can easily squeeze you in." He then asks each of his current guests to move from their current room to the next one along. The guest in room 1 moves to room 2; the guest in room 2 moves to room 3; and so on.

A CHALLENGE

Imagine you are the manager of Hilbert's Hotel. Every room is occupied. Ten new guests arrive. How can you accommodate them?

SOLUTION
Move the guest in room 1 to room 11, the guest in room 2 to room 12, and so on.

Original room: 1 2 3 4 5 6 7…

New room: 2 3 4 5 6 7 8…

Room 1 is now unoccupied, and the newcomer can be accommodated.

94

A Bigger Problem at Hilbert's Hotel

The extra guest has now been successfully accommodated at the still fully occupied Hilbert's Hotel. Until, that is, the poor manager is faced with an even bigger challenge. An infinite number of new guests arrive. "No problem," he says, after a moment's thought. "All I need to do is jiggle things around a bit."

He then asks each of the existing guests to move to the room number that's double the one they're currently in. The occupant of room 1 moves to room 2; the occupant of room 2 moves to room 4; and so on.

Original room: 1 2 3 4 5 6 7...

New room: 2 4 6 8 10 12 14...

This frees up the odd-numbered rooms to accommodate the infinite number of new arrivals.

An Even Bigger Problem at Hilbert's Hotel

An infinite number of infinitely large tour groups arrive at the fully occupied Hilbert's Hotel. This gives our beleaguered hotel manager pause for thought. But, after some head-scratching, he realizes that he can still accommodate all of the new arrivals.

He moves all of his existing guests into rooms that are powers of the lowest prime number: two. So that's 2, 4, 8, 16, 32...

Then he moves the first tour group into rooms that are powers of the next prime number: three. So that's 3, 9, 27, 81, 243...

After that, he moves the second tour group into rooms that are multiples of the next prime number: five. That's 5, 25, 125, 625, 3125...

He then continues to assign tour groups to room numbers that are powers of successive prime numbers. Since there are an infinite number of primes (see pp. 84–85), an infinite number of infinitely large tour groups can thus be accommodated.

This system of allocating rooms leaves many rooms unoccupied. So the manager's solution is rather inefficient. But at least that leaves plenty of room for new arrivals!

Bigger Infinities: Part 1

According to Cantor, two infinite sets have the same cardinality, or size, if their elements can be placed in a one-to-one correspondence with one another.

Counting Fractions

All infinite sets of whole numbers can be placed in a one-to-one correspondence with one another, and therefore have the same cardinality. But what about fractions?

Consider the infinite set of rational numbers (the fractions that can be formed by dividing one whole number by another). It is difficult to imagine that these could ever be placed into a one-to-one correspondence with the natural numbers, since between any two whole numbers we can always cram in as many fractions as we like.

Yet Cantor demonstrated that there is a one-to-one correspondence. The trick is to find a nice, ordered way of listing the rational numbers, so that none of them get missed out. Here's how he did it.

$\frac{1}{1}$
$\frac{2}{1}$, $\frac{1}{2}$
$\frac{3}{1}$, $\frac{2}{2}$, $\frac{1}{3}$
$\frac{4}{1}$, $\frac{3}{2}$, $\frac{2}{3}$, $\frac{1}{4}$
$\frac{5}{1}$, $\frac{4}{2}$, $\frac{3}{3}$, $\frac{2}{4}$, $\frac{1}{5}$
$\frac{6}{1}$, $\frac{5}{2}$, $\frac{4}{3}$, $\frac{3}{4}$, $\frac{2}{5}$, $\frac{1}{6}$
$\frac{7}{1}$, $\frac{6}{2}$, … and so on.

CHALLENGE 1

Show that the set of natural numbers has the same cardinality as the set of even numbers by placing their elements in a one-to-one correspondence.

SOLUTION
Naturals: 1 2 3 4 5 6 7 8…
Evens: 2 4 6 8 10 12 14 16…

CHALLENGE 2

Now do the same thing for the natural numbers and the integers greater than 1.

SOLUTION
Naturals: 1 2 3 4 5 6 7 8…
Integers >1: 2 3 4 5 6 7 8 9…

This explains why there is always room for another guest at Hilbert's Hotel (see pp. 94–95).

It's a simple but elegant method. The first row contains those fractions whose numerator and denominator add up to two (1+1); the second row contains fractions whose numerator and denominator add up to three (2+1, 1+2); in the third row the total is always 4 (3+1, 2+2, 1+3); and so on.

Now it is simplicity itself to demonstrate one-to-one correspondence with the natural numbers. Just plow through the rationals, row by row:

Naturals: 1 2 3 4 5

Rationals: ⅟₁ ²⁄₁ ½ ³⁄₁ ²⁄₂

The duplications (for example, ⅟₁ = 2⁄2) need not bother us. We could simply skip the duplicate fractions, if we so desired. So, although we might have suspected that there are vastly more fractions than whole numbers, it turns out that they are equinumerous.

Countable Infinities

Now for a definition: an infinite set whose members can be paired off neatly with the natural numbers is said to be denumerable, or countable. All of the infinite sets we have considered so far, including the fractions, have been shown to be countable.

So, are all infinite sets countable? Or do non-countable, hence bigger, infinities exist? Turn the page to find out.

CHALLENGE 3

We have already seen that it is a simple matter to place the odd and even numbers in a one-to-one correspondence with one another (see p. 91). The same goes for the natural and square numbers. But here is a trickier problem. Try to show that the natural numbers (1, 2, 3, 4, 5...) can be placed in a one-to-one correspondence with the set comprising the positive and negative integers and zero (...–3, –2, –1, 0, 1, 2, 3...).

SOLUTION

The trick is to start at zero and then bounce backward and forward. Like this:

Naturals: 1 2 3 4 5 6 7 8...

-ve, 0, +ve: 0 1 –1 2 –2 3 –3 4...

Congratulations if you worked that one out for yourself. You've got talent!

Bigger Infinities: Part 2

Once Cantor had demonstrated that the infinity of fractions is countable he turned his attention to the decimals. The set of decimals includes not only the rational numbers, but also the irrationals (those that cannot be represented by fractions). Many decimals are never-ending.

After a great deal of hard work, Cantor came up with a brilliant proof that the decimals are, in fact, uncountable. He did this by means of a reductio ad absurdum (see pp. 84–85). Here's how.

Begin with the assumption that the decimals are countable, which means that they can be paired off neatly with the infinity of natural numbers. For example:

1   0.54354349...
2   0.84920018...
3   0.68872574...
4   0.58823161...
    ...and so on,
    ad infinitum.

Only the first eight digits of each decimal are shown, and the order is random. The important point is that, since the decimals are in a one-to-one correspondence with the natural numbers, none of the decimals are left out. The sequence includes all of them.

Here comes the clever bit. It is now possible to construct a new decimal that's not in the existing sequence. Here's how.

Begin by choosing a first digit that differs from the first digit of the first decimal in the sequence (for example, a 6 instead of a 5). Then choose a second digit that differs from the second digit of the second decimal (say, a 5 instead of a 4). And so on, and so on. This produces a never-ending decimal that differs from every item in the existing sequence by at least one digit.

Thus we have a contradiction. The initial assumption of one-to-one correspondence meant that the sequence was supposed to contain all of the decimals. But then we constructed another one! The initial assumption was therefore wrong, which means that the decimals cannot be paired off with the naturals. They are uncountable.

Bigger Infinities

This is amazing. Paradoxical even. Our intuition tells us that nothing is bigger than infinity. But Cantor has demonstrated that the infinity of decimals is bigger than the infinity of natural numbers. Indeed they represent a whole higher order of infinity, infinitely bigger than any countable infinity.

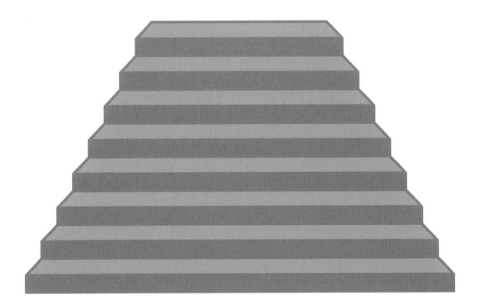

Bigger and Bigger Infinities

But it doesn't stop there. Cantor went on to show that there is an even bigger infinity that can't be put into one-to-one correspondence with the decimals. And then there's another, still larger, infinity that can't be put into one-to-one correspondence with that one. And so on, and so on, ad infinitum.

To appreciate how this works, we can begin by considering a finite set containing just three objects, say {Monica, Rachel, Phoebe}, and asking ourselves how many subsets it has.

It is no difficult matter to see that there are eight subsets: the empty set {Ø}; the set itself {Monica, Rachel, Phoebe}; all the different pairings {Monica, Rachel}, {Monica, Phoebe}, {Rachel, Phoebe}; plus all the singles {Monica}, {Rachel} and {Phoebe}. So, from a set containing three elements, we can form a bigger

"power set" (the set of subsets of that set) containing eight elements.

It turns out that for any set, whether finite or infinite, we can always form a power set that's bigger than the set itself. This is how Cantor constructs his never-ending hierarchy of infinities. At the bottom are the countable infinities such as the natural numbers; next-up are the decimals; and so it continues, up and up, forever.

Cantor's Paradox

Given any set, you can always form a power set that's bigger than the set itself. But this gives rise to a paradox when you consider the universal set: the set of all sets.

The universal set surely ought to be the biggest of all sets. Yet its power set is even bigger. So the universal set both is, and is not, the biggest set of all. Hence there cannot be a universal set.

Exercise 4

Richard's Paradox

THE PROBLEM:

Cantor's diagonal argument is implicated in many famous paradoxes. You have seen it at work in the proof that there are uncountably many "real numbers" ("decimals" as defined on p. 98, *Bigger Infinities*). See if you can apply the diagonal method to prove the paradox about real numbers known as the *Richard Paradox*:

"The set of real numbers definable in finitely many words is both denumerable and non-denumerable, countable and uncountable."

THE METHOD:

First show the set is denumerable by giving an enumeration, or infinite listing, of all the finitely long definitions of real numbers. Then use the diagonal method to construct a finitely long definition of a real number not in that list.

Start with some definitions. The set of real numbers is the set of all rational and irrational numbers. (The rational numbers are those that can be expressed as fractions. The irrational are finite numbers that cannot be so expressed; think of pi=π=3.1415926…, which is equal to no fraction or ratio of two whole numbers.) Using his famous diagonal argument, Cantor was able to prove that the set of real numbers (unlike the set of all fractions) is uncountable or non-denumerable, meaning

that it could not be put into a one-to-one correspondence with the set of whole or counting numbers $\{1, 2, 3, \ldots\}$. The set of real numbers is therefore larger than any countably infinite (or denumerable) set.

To solve this puzzle, you will need to define the concept "definable in finitely many words." We can assume words of the English language are intended, which are all spelled in the English alphabet. So any defining phrase in English will have some finite number of words, and phrases of the same number of words can be put into alphabetical order. For instance, all one-word definitions of real numbers might be listed alphabetically in one column, all two-word definitions of real numbers listed alphabetically in an adjacent column to the right, then all three-word definitions in a column next to that, and so on.

It is easy to show from here that the set FR={the set of real numbers definable in finitely many English words}, though infinite, is countable. Hint: use a table method similar to that used to show the countability of the set of all fractions (which can also be arranged in an infinite table like the one just described—see p. 98, *Bigger Infinities*). For a solution, see (1) below.

More difficult is to show the opposite. Having demonstrated that all the finitely long definitions are in the enumeration, you now use the diagonal method to construct a finitely long definition of a real number not on your list.

Suppose your enumeration of finitely long definitions has produced a list of definitions of real numbers:

$$D_1, D_2, D_3, ..., D_n, ...$$

Each of these defining phrases, which has only finitely many words, defines a real number:

$$r_1, r_2, r_3, ..., r_n, ...$$

Each of these real numbers can be represented as an infinite decimal expansion (possibly consisting of only 0s after some decimal place). Now consider that each real number R_k in this list has in the kth decimal place of its decimal expansion some whole number n (where $0 \pi n \pi 9$). Using Cantor's diagonal method, and finitely many words, define (the infinite decimal expansion of) a real number RR(=Richards's Real number) so that it cannot be identical to any of the real numbers listed above.

Hint: Define the kth decimal place of RR in such a way that RR$\neq r_k$, for any k.

THE SOLUTION:
(1) FR is denumerable, or countably infinite.
To show that FR is a denumerable set, it suffices to list all the finitely long definitions. Starting from the infinite array of alphabetical columns described in the text, begin to list the definitions $D_1, D_2, D_3, ... D_n, ...$a zig-zag motion through the table, thus:

1	2	6	7	...
3	5	8	14	
4	9	13		
10	12			
11				

(2) FR is non-denumerable, or uncountably infinite.
It suffices to define (the infinite decimal expansion of) RR as follows:

Let the kth decimal place of RR = n+1, where n is the number in the kth decimal place of the r_k, for any k; except where n = 9, then let the kth decimal place of RR = 0.

It will follow that RR$\neq r_k$, for any k, because it will differ from r_k at the kth decimal place.

However, the above definition is in English, or could readily be rendered into a finitely long English phrase, so it must be D_j, for some *j*. From this the contradiction apparently follows:

$$rj = RR \neq rj.$$

The paradox is named for its discoverer, Jules Richard.

Chapter 5

Probability Paradoxes

Chances are you too have made common errors of statistical reasoning. We look at some of the most frequently occurring fallacies of probabilistic thinking, then up the ante by tackling a few of the odds-on favorite probability paradoxes of all time. We play dice in this chapter, ask what's likely to be behind closed doors, and place cosmic wagers, all in a double effort to see probability as paradoxical and probability paradoxes as paradoxically probable.

The Gambler's Fallacy

Many of the paradoxes in this chapter are concerned with probability. So, to begin with, here's a brief introduction to the mathematics involved.

Probabilities are numbers between 0 and 1 that tell us how likely various events are. An event that will certainly happen, such as the sun rising tomorrow, has a probability of 1. An event that will certainly not happen, such as throwing a seven on a standard dice, has probability 0. An event that is equally likely to happen or not, such as tossing "heads" on a fair coin, has a probability of 0.5. Alternatively, probabilities can be expressed as fractions or percentages.

Of course, we can't be completely certain that the sun will rise tomorrow (see the problem of induction on p. 29). But in this chapter we will lay aside such skeptical doubts.

To calculate the probability of an event, we divide the ways it can happen by the total number of possible outcomes (assuming that all outcomes are equally likely).

For example, what is the probability of throwing a four on a single throw of a fair dice? Well, there are six numbers on a dice, all equally likely to be thrown, and only one of them is a four. So the probability is ⅙ or 0.16.

How about the probability of throwing an even number? Well there are three even numbers (two, four, and six) out of six numbers overall. So the probability is ³⁄₆, which simplifies to ½, or 0.5, or 50%.

LIGHTNING STRIKES TWICE

The chances of being struck by lightning, once in a given year, are about one in 650,000. If Elektra is struck by lightning in 2009, what are the chances she will be struck by lightning in 2010?

SOLUTION

Lightning strikes are independent events. Therefore the chances are still one in 650,000. Being struck by lightning in one year doesn't make you any more or less likely to be struck in the next... unless of course the first strike kills you!

The Gambler's Fallacy

There is a very common belief that random events will even themselves out over time. So, for example, if red comes up ten times in a row on a roulette wheel, punters will begin betting on black in the belief that a run of blacks is due. Similarly, if a fair coin is tossed repeatedly, and there's a run of say seven tails, many people will think that the next toss will very likely be heads—to redress the balance.

This erroneous belief is known as the Gambler's Fallacy. The truth of the matter is that the chances of a fair coin turning up heads on any particular toss are even (0.5) regardless of what's gone on before. This is because coin tosses are independent events: they have no bearing on one another.

DRAWING ACES

There are 52 playing cards, excluding jokers, in a standard deck. Four of them are aces. The probability of drawing an ace is therefore $^4/_{52}$, which simplifies to $^1/_{13}$. Doc Holliday shuffles a fair deck and pulls out a card at random. It's the ace of spades. He places it on the table, shuffles the rest of the pack, and pulls out another card. What are the chances that it too is an ace?

SOLUTION

If Doc Holliday had replaced the ace of spades before reshuffling the deck, then the probability would still be $^1/_{13}$. The mere fact of having drawn an ace first time around has no bearing on the chances on the second one second time around.

But this case is different since Doc Holliday removes the ace of spades from the pack before reshuffling. This leaves only three remaining aces among 51 remaining cards. So the chances of drawing an ace are now $^3/_{51}$, which simplifies to $^1/_{17}$. In this case, the first and second card-draws are not independent events.

105

Girls and Boys

This entertaining puzzle demonstrates just how easy it is to go astray when estimating or calculating probabilities.

The Family Smith

Mr. and Mrs. Smith have two children, at least one of whom is a girl. What are the chances that the other child is a girl too? Think carefully before answering.

Since this is a book about paradoxes—and you've been warned to be careful—you probably suspect some kind of trick. But there isn't one. It's a perfectly straightforward question. The mystery child is quite definitely a boy or a girl (not, say, a hermaphrodite), and you can assume that the two genders are equally common. No tricks. So, what are the chances that the other child is a girl?

It's perfectly obvious to almost everyone that the chances are even. After all, the chances that any child is a girl are even. So how can the gender of a sibling make any difference?

Unfortunately, the "obvious" answer is wrong. The correct answer is one in three.

Here's why:

When it comes to the gender of two children, we must consider four possible permutations: both of them can be boys; both of them can be girls; the first one can be a boy and the second a girl; or the first can be a girl and the second a boy. We can write this as: BB, GG, BG, and GB.

We know that at least one of the Smith children is a girl. So that puts BB out of the running. This leaves us with three equally likely alternatives: GG, BG, and GB. Only one (GG) of those three possibilities makes both of the Smith children girls. So the probability that the "other" child is a girl is one in three, or ⅓.

This is a paradox only in the weakest sense, in that it runs counter to our intuitions. But it does illustrate just how fallible our intuitions are when it comes to estimating or calculating probabilities, even in very straightforward situations.

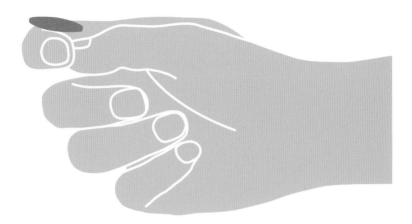

HEADS 'N' TAILS

A gambler tossed three fair coins. At least two of them came up heads. What are the chances that the other one came up heads too?

SOLUTION

First, resist the urge to shout "even!" Then write out all of the permutations for three coin tosses: HHH, HTH, HTT, TTH, THT, TTH, and TTT. That's eight, in all. Four of those permutations contain two or more heads: HHH, HHT, HTH, and THH; and out of those, only one (HHH) contains the additional heads we require. Therefore the answer is one in four or ¼.

The Family Jones

Here's a similar situation in which Mr. and Mrs. Jones have two children, the eldest of whom is a girl. What are the chances that the second child is a girl too? Think carefully before you answer.

Hopefully you didn't fall into the trap I set for you. This time the answer really is even. Here's why:

Once again, we're dealing with four permutations: BB, GG, BG, and GB. But this time, because we know that the eldest child is a girl, we can discount two of them: BB and BG.

The remaining options are GG and GB. Only one of these makes the youngest child a girl. So that makes the chances one in two, or ½.

The crucial difference between this puzzle and the last is that this time we are given additional information. Instead of being told merely that one of the children is a girl, we are told specifically that the eldest child is a girl.

Shared Birthdays

What are the chances that two people, chosen at random, share the same birthday?

This is a straightforward puzzle with a straightforward solution. Let's assume that one of those people has a birthday on, say, March 15. There are 365 days in a year, and only one of those is March 15. So the chances that the second person shares that birthday are $\frac{1}{365}$ (roughly 0.003). (For the sake of simplicity, we will ignore leap year birthdays throughout this section.)

The Birthday Problem

Here's a rather more interesting puzzle, which is often referred to as the Birthday Problem. How large a group of people do you need before you have an even chance (or better) that two of them will share a birthday? Consider this for a moment before reading on.

With 365 birthday slots to fill, most people guess that you need quite a large group. When I put this question to my friends and family I got answers ranging from 180 to 366.

In fact, calculation shows the correct answer to be 23—a result so mind-bogglingly low that some people flatly refuse to belief it. We will examine the calculation in a moment. But first; some background mathematics.

Combining Probabilities

When we toss a fair coin there are just two possible outcomes: heads and tails. So the probability that the coin will land on heads is one in two, or $\frac{1}{2}$. But what if we toss

the same coin twice, or toss two different coins? What are the chances of heads turning up both times?

The two coin tosses are independent events. In other words, one event has no bearing on the other event. In such cases we calculate the combined probability simply by multiplying the individual probabilities together.

So the probability of getting two heads in a row is $\frac{1}{2} \times \frac{1}{2} = \frac{1}{4}$. Similarly, the probability of getting three heads in a row is $\frac{1}{2} \times \frac{1}{2} \times \frac{1}{2} = \frac{1}{8}$; and so on.

Here's another example. Suppose we throw a fair dice and we toss a fair coin. What are the chances that the dice will land on six and the coin turn up heads? To find out, we simply multiply the probability of throwing a six by the probability of tossing heads. That's $\frac{1}{6} \times \frac{1}{2} = \frac{1}{12}$.

The Birthday Problem: Calculation

Now we have enough background information to tackle the Birthday Problem. Obviously, in a "group" containing just one person there's a probability of 0 that two people will share a birthday. Whereas in a group containing 366 people we are certain to have a shared birthday; so that's a probability of 1.

What we want to know is how large a group of people we need before we have an even chance, or better, that two of them will share a birthday. The easiest way to calculate this is to first ask ourselves a related question: how likely is it that the members of a group do not share a birthday?

Consider a group with just two people. The first person's birthday can be on any day of the year. But in order not to clash with the first person's birthday, the second person's birthday must fall on one of the remaining 364 days. So the probability that two people won't share a birthday is $^{364}/_{365}$.

When a third person joins the group there are 363 free days remaining. So she has a $^{363}/_{365}$ chance of her birthday not clashing with the first two. For a fourth person, the chances of not sharing a birthday are $^{362}/_{365}$. For a fifth person the odds are $^{361}/_{365}$. And so on, and so on.

This means that the combined probability that, say, a group of five

people don't share any birthdays is $(^{364}/_{365})$ x $(^{363}/_{365})$ x $(^{362}/_{365})$ x $(^{361}/_{365})$, which works out at about 0.973.

If you perform the same calculation for 23 people, the probability that they don't share a birthday is about 0.492. The probability that they do share a birthday is therefore $1 - 0.492 = 0.508$. Thus, once we get to 23 people, we have just over an even chance that two of them will share a birthday.

The Birthday Paradox

This problem is sometimes referred to as the Birthday Paradox. Of course, it's a paradox only in the weakest sense, in that it runs counter to our common sense intuition. But it demonstrates, once again, just how fallible our intuitions are when it comes to estimating probabilities.

The Monty Hall Problem: Part 1

There are few puzzles that give rise to as much bafflement, incredulity, brain-ache, and plain old-fashioned ill-temper as this one. I first stumbled across it in Mark Haddon's best-selling 2003 novel, *The Curious Incident of the Dog in the Night-Time*.

For days, I worried and fretted about it, because even though the author gave the correct solution, and even though I could see that his math was unimpeachable, it still didn't make any darn sense!

My eureka moment finally arrived while I was lying in the bathtub. I resisted the temptation to "do an Archimedes" and run naked through the streets of my hometown. But only just. If you've never seen this puzzle, and value your sanity, you may want to skip to p.114.

Cars 'n' Goats

Imagine you are the winning contestant on a game show. In the show's nail-biting climax, you get to open one of three doors and keep whatever's behind it. Behind one of the doors is a brand-new car; and behind each of the others is a goat.

You make your choice. At this point, according to the rules of the game, the host must open one of the other two doors and reveal a goat. He does this, and then gives you the option of swapping your chosen door for the remaining one.

The question is: should you stick with your original door, swap to the other one, or doesn't it make any difference?

Stop and think. Is there any advantage in swapping? Think carefully about this before reading on. Take your time. This satanically fiendish puzzle has claimed countless victims.

The Obvious Solution

The solution to this puzzle seems blindingly obvious. There are two remaining doors. One of them conceals a car, the other a goat. Simple. Therefore it doesn't matter a jot whether you swap or not. Either way, there's an even chance of winning the car, and an even chance of walking away with a goat.

But this is a book about paradoxes. So, predictably, I have to inform you that the blindingly obvious solution is incorrect. Incredible as it may seem, swapping really does make a difference. In fact, swapping doubles your chances of winning the car.

The Great Debate

In September 1990, in an issue of *Parade* magazine, High-IQ columnist Marilyn vos Savant introduced this puzzle in the weekly "Ask Marilyn" section.

The puzzle was based on the T.V. show, *Let's Make a Deal*, in which host Monty Hall presented contestants with essentially the same choices in order to win either a high-value prize or one of two undesirable alternatives (referred to as "zonks").

Marilyn's analysis revealed, quite correctly, that switching doors doubles the chances of driving away a shiny new car. But readers wrote in their thousands to disagree. Many of her severest critics were people with math and science Ph.D.s, who hauled her over the coals for what they considered a monumental gaffe.

The debate raged for almost a year, culminating in a front-page article in the *New York Times* on Sunday, July 21, 1991, in which Marilyn's analysis was vindicated.

STRAIN YOUR BRAIN

If you have never encountered the Monty Hall problem before, you are probably baffled as to how the swapping doors strategy works. You'll find out on the next page (although you might not believe it).

In the meantime, see if you can succeed where scores of math professors and scientists failed. Try to work out for yourself why swapping doors improves your chances.

The Monty Hall Problem: Part 2

Marilyn vos Savant's response to the Monty Hall Problem was so counterintuitive that many people, including many professional mathematicians, couldn't accept it.

In order to understand why Marilyn got it right while so many others got it wrong, it will be helpful to attack the problem from two different sides: for the case where you don't swap doors; and for the case where you do.

Your Chances When You Don't Swap?

Initially you are asked to choose one of three doors. Behind one door there's a car; behind the others there are goats. Each door is equally likely to conceal the car. Therefore the probability that you will choose correctly are one in three, or ⅓.

Whether you pick the correct door or not, the game-show host will always be able to open a door with a goat behind it. So, in doing so, he provides no further clue about whether your initial choice is right or wrong.

Let's say your initial choice is correct. Then not swapping wins you a brand-new, shiny car.

Let's say your initial choice is incorrect. Then your refusal to swap wins you a goat.

But remember: you only had a one-in-three chance of choosing correctly first time, compared to a two-in-three chance of choosing incorrectly. So—just to hammer it home—if you don't swap, the probability of winning the car is ⅓.

Your Chances When You Do Swap?

When you make your initial choice, you have a one-in-three chance of picking the car.

Let's say your initial choice is correct. Then swapping loses you the car. Unlucky!

Let's say your initial choice is incorrect. In that case, the car is hidden behind one of the remaining doors. But the game-show host helpfully eliminates the one with the goat for you. So swapping nets you a car.

So there's a one-in-three chance that your initial choice was correct, in which case swapping loses you the car. But there's a two-in-three chance that your initial choice was incorrect, in which case swapping wins you the car.

So swapping bumps up your chances of winning to ⅔!

Why It's So Hard to Believe

The correct solution is so utterly counterintuitive that the Monty Hall Problem is often referred to as the Monty Hall Paradox. It seems blindingly obvious to almost everyone that swapping doors can confer no advantage. And yet it does. Even when the correct analysis is given, people find it very difficult to accept. Why so?

The problem, I think, is that you end up with a choice between two doors, each of which seems equally likely to conceal a car. But, in fact, the probabilities are not equal. Assuming that your first choice was incorrect (which it will be ⅔ of the time), the host has no choice but to eliminate the goat from the remaining prizes. Obviously, this works to your advantage.

SEE FOR YOURSELF

If you find my analysis unconvincing, please don't write and tell me that I'm wrong. Instead, try playing a simulation of the Monty Hall problem. There are many animated versions on the Internet, including a really nice one on the *New York Times* website. (Just search for "New York Times Monty Hall.")

You'll find that in the long run you'll win the car just $\frac{1}{3}$ of the time if you adopt a "never swap" strategy, but $\frac{2}{3}$ of the time if you adopt an "always swap" strategy.

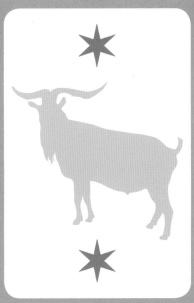

The Two-Envelope Paradox: Part 1

This awesome paradox was devised by the great German mathematician Edmund Landau (1877–1938). And it takes us a step closer to genuine paradox than the Monty Hall Problem discussed on the previous pages.

Two Envelopes

Imagine that you are once more the winning contestant on a game show. You get to choose between two sealed envelopes, A and B, and keep the contents. You are told that each envelope contains a check, and that one is worth double the other.

Of course, the choice of envelope is arbitrary. But the game-show host asks the studio audience to help you choose, and there are loud cries of "A" and "B," in equal proportions.

Tentatively, you reach out and take envelope A. There are cheers and groans from the audience. When the noise dies down, the host asks, "Before you open your envelope, would you like to swap it for the other one?"

Could there be any advantage in swapping? Think about this before reading on.

Common sense says there's absolutely no point swapping. After all, the chances are even that you've already chosen the envelope with the largest check. If you decide to swap, the odds will be no better. So why torture yourself?

You look up at the host and say, "No, thanks. I'll stick with envelope A."

On Second Thought...

"I'll tell you what," says the host, casting a mischievous sideways glance at the studio audience, why don't you take a peek inside your envelope—and then decide.

Slowly, you peel open the envelope… and pull out a check for $10,000. The audience breaks into applause. The host smiles archly and says, "Now would you like to swap?"

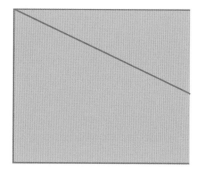

You are about to refuse, but then a thought occurs to you. If you do swap, then you'll either get half of $10,000 ($5,000) or double $10,000 ($20,000). So, although you stand to lose $5,000, you also stand to gain $10,000.

It's beginning to look like you ought to swap.

You decide to think through the calculations more carefully. You currently have $10,000. If you swap then you have a 0.5 chance of getting $5000 and a 0.5 chance of getting $20,000. So the expected value of the swap is $(0.5 \times \$5000) + (0.5 \times \$20,000) = \$12,500$, which gives you an expected gain of $2,500, or 25%.

Clearly, then, you ought to swap.

In fact, you needn't even have looked at the contents of your envelope to decide this. Whatever amount is in your envelope, say x dollars, it is always worthwhile swapping. Here's why:

You'll either make a bad swap and get 0.5x dollars, or a good swap and get 2x dollars. So, on average, you can expect to walk away with $(0.5 \times \$0.5x) + (0.5 \times \$2x) = 1.25x$. The expected gain is 25%, regardless of the amount in your envelope.

The Paradox

But hang on a moment. This is absurd. You were given a random choice between two envelopes. How can it possibly be advantageous to choose one and then switch to the other?

Look at it another way. Your first choice was completely arbitrary; it could just as easily have been envelope B that you chose. And if it had been envelope B, precisely the same process of reasoning would have dictated swapping from B to A.

This, then, is the paradox. Common sense says it can't possibly make any difference to swap. But our carefully reasoned probability argument indicates that it does.

Will the victory go to common sense, or to our probability argument? Do you still think there's no advantage in swapping? Turn the page to find out.

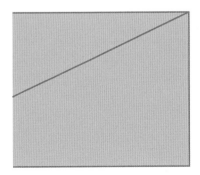

The Two-Envelope Paradox: Part 2

In the Two-Envelope Paradox we've just seen that common sense assures us that there's no advantage in swapping envelopes, whereas an apparently valid probability argument says there is.

An Alternative Analysis

Here's another, perhaps simpler, way of analyzing the problem. There are two envelopes, A and B. Both of them contain checks, and one check is for double the amount of the other.

Let's say that one envelope contains $x, and the other $2x. In this case, a lucky swap will net you an extra $x, whereas an unlucky swap will lose you $x. You are just as likely to have picked either envelope initially. So you have an even chance of winning or losing $x. Everything's perfectly symmetrical.

The expected value of swapping is $(0.5 \times \$x) + (0.5 \times \$2x) = \$1.5x$. The expected value of not swapping is $(0.5 \times \$x) + (0.5 \times \$2x) = \$1.5x$. So, again, the situation is perfectly symmetrical.

Therefore there's no advantage to be gained by swapping—a result that accords nicely with common sense.

It seems, then, that there has to be something wrong with our previous probability argument. But what is it?

The Flaw in the Probability Argument

To identify the flaw in the probability argument, it will be helpful to reconsider the Two-Envelope Paradox for the special case where there's a finite prize-fund, say $1,000.

Now, according to the probability argument, there's always an even chance that envelope B contains twice as much as A. Equally, there's always an even chance that B contains half as much as A. But with a total prize-fund of $1000, this is clearly not the case.

Suppose you open envelope A and find $600 inside. Clearly there's no chance at all that envelope B contains twice as much, since $1,200 would exceed the prize-fund. This means that envelope B must contain just $300.

In fact, if envelope A contains anything over $500 then envelope B definitely contains half as much rather than twice as much.

More generally, if the total prize-fund is $y, and envelope A contains more than $y/2, then envelope B definitely contains the smaller amount.

Notice that y can be any finite amount. Therefore, for any finite amount, it is simply not true to say that there's always an even chance that envelope B contains twice as much as A.

A Simple Illustration

To illustrate what happens in a two-envelope game with finite prizes, let's consider a very simple setup in which the total prize fund is $8, and in which each envelope can only contain whole-dollar amounts. Here are all of the possibilities, set out in table form.

A Contains	B Contains	Swapping A for B
$1	$2	Gains $1
$2	$4	Gains $2
$2	$1	Loses $1
$3	$6	Gains $3
$4	$8	Gains $4
$4	$2	Loses $2
$6	$3	Loses $3
$8	$4	Loses $4

Net gain: $0

Clearly, the losses and gains associated with swapping cancel one another out. Therefore swapping confers no advantage.

Finite versus Infinite Prizes

Losses and gains cancel out like this for any two-envelope game involving finite prizes. The assumption that there's always an even chance that B contains twice A, and always an even chance that B contains half A, simply isn't true in such cases.

So, when there's a finite prize-limit, the paradox disappears.

What about when the money supply is infinite? In that case, the paradox seems to hold. But as we learned repeatedly throughout Chapter 4, infinity is a very strange beast.

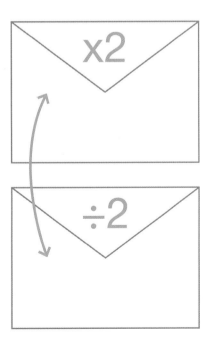

The St. Petersburg Paradox

In the eighteenth century, the Russian capital, St. Petersburg, was a leading center for mathematics, and attracted gifted mathematicians from all over Europe. It was there that Swiss cousins Nicholas and Daniel Bernoulli developed what has become known as the St. Petersburg Paradox.

The Toss of a Coin

Imagine you are invited to gamble on a game of chance, played according to the following rules:

A fair coin is tossed repeatedly until it comes up heads, at which point the game ends. If heads comes up on the first toss, you win $1. If it doesn't come up until the second toss, you win $2. If it doesn't come up until the third toss, you win $4. And so on, and so on, with the payout doubling each time.

In general, if the coin turns up heads on the nth toss, you win 2^{n-1} dollars, and the game ends.

How much would you be willing to pay to play this game?

What's It Worth?

To decide what would be a reasonable stake for a game of chance, you must first calculate what the game is worth: its expected value.

Say, for example, you are given the opportunity to gamble on the outcome of a single toss of a fair coin. You are offered $10 should the coin land on heads, and $2 should it land on tails. In that case, you have a 0.5 chance of winning $10, and a 0.5 chance of winning $2. The expected value of the game is therefore (0.5 x $10) + (0.5 x $2) = $6.

Since the game is worth $6, you'd be justified in paying anything up to $6 to play. If you were able to stake just $4 there'd be a strong motivation to play, since your expected gain would be $6 – $4 = $2.

So what about the St. Petersburg game? How do we calculate its expected value?

Well, there's a 0.5 chance that the coin will turn up heads on the very first toss, in which case you'll win $1. So that possibility is worth 0.5 x $1 = $0.5.

And then there's a 0.5 x 0.5 chance that the coin will land first on tails and then on heads, in which case you'll win $2. So that possibility is worth 0.5 x 0.5 x $2 = $0.5.

And then there's a 0.5 x 0.5 x 0.5 chance that you'll get two tails followed by a heads, in which case you'll win $4. So that possibility is worth 0.5 x 0.5 x 0.5 x $4 = $0.5.

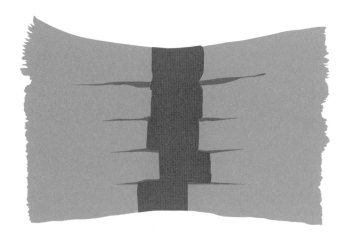

Clearly, there's no end to these possible outcomes, each of which has half the probability of the previous one but double the prize. So the total expected value of the game is: 0.5 + 0.5 + 0.5 +...+ 0.5... dollars. In other words, the game has an infinite expected value.

How much would you be justified in staking on a game like this, with an infinite expected value? Surely, any amount. And yet you'd probably hesitate to stake a mere $100, wouldn't you?

Resolving the Paradox

The St. Petersburg Paradox is a genuine one in that its contradictory conclusion (the game has infinite expected value, yet you wouldn't stake much on it) results from valid reasoning. There is no universally agreed resolution, but here are some common responses. Which do you find appealing?

1. Money is finite: The expected value of the game is supposed to be infinite, but there's a finite amount of money in the world. In practice, then, the expected value of the game is finite.

2. Diminishing returns: Doubling the amount of prize money doesn't double its value. Winning $10 billion is a wonderful thing. Winning $20 billion is a wonderful thing too. But it isn't twice as wonderful. In terms of actual value, money is subject to the law of diminishing returns. So although cash prizes double every time an additional "tails" is thrown, the value of those prizes doesn't.

3. Huge prizes are rare: The odds of winning a huge prize are very small. It's far more likely that you'll win only a modest one. Whatever the math says, there's nothing irrational about refusing to gamble a hefty stake on a low-probability outcome.

Profile

Blaise Pascal

The achievements of the French mathematician, scientist, and theologian, Blaise Pascal (1623–1662) are so numerous that a superficial biography can scarcely do him justice.

Aged just 18, he designed and built an arithmetic machine to help his father with the calculations he had to do as a tax commissioner. In honor of this achievement, the computer programming language PASCAL was named after him.

Later, Pascal turned his attention to the science of hydrostatics. He did groundbreaking work in vacuum physics; invented the syringe; and formulated what has become known as Pascal's law, which states that when pressure is applied to a contained fluid the force is transmitted equally in all directions. The SI unit for pressure is known as the pascal (Pa).

He was also a first-rate mathematician. In 1653 he wrote an important Treatise on the Arithmetical Triangle, which every schoolchild now knows as "Pascal's triangle."

In 1654, Pascal became interested in the application of mathematics to games of chance. His resulting collaboration with Pierre de Fermat gave birth to the mathematical theory of probabilities. Hence, Pascal is considered to be the founding father of probability theory.

In fact, the notion of expected value, discussed on pp. 118–119, originated with Pascal.

Pascal's Wager

Late in 1654, Pascal had a mystical experience so profound and intense that he abandoned science and devoted himself to theology instead. His most important work from this period is a defense of the Christian faith, entitled *Pensées* (or *Thoughts*). This was unfinished when he died, and had to be pieced together from various notes he left behind.

The *Pensées* contains one of the most famous arguments in the philosophy of religion, in which Pascal applies probability theory to the practical question of whether one ought to believe in God.

Pascal's jottings leave the precise form of the argument open to interpretation. But it is usually presented along the following lines.

You are undecided about whether to believe in God. Like a gambler who must call "heads" or "tails," you do not know how to choose. Very well, then the sensible thing to do is to compare the expected value of believing with the expected value of not believing. Then you will know which option is most prudent.

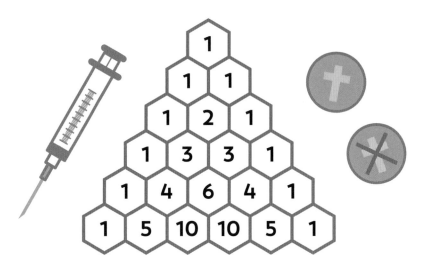

What is the expected value of believing? Well, if God exists, he will grant you eternal bliss; whereas if He does not exist, you will lose a finite amount of worldly pleasure. Now, infinity minus a finite amount equals infinity. Therefore the expected value of believing is infinite.

What is the expected value of not believing? Well, if God exists, He may punish you with eternal damnation; whereas if He does not exist, you will gain a finite amount of worldly pleasure. So the rewards of not believing are small, at best.

Clearly, therefore, prudence dictates that you choose the believing option.

Interestingly, the wager argument recommends that you believe in God even if you think His existence is unlikely.

Say, for example, you think there's only a thousand-to-one chance (0.001) that God exists. Nevertheless, there's an infinite reward if your gamble on Him pays off. In that case, the expected value of believing in God equals the probability that He exists (0.001) multiplied by the reward you'll receive if

He does exist (which is infinite). Now, any number, however small, times infinity equals infinity. Therefore, if you choose to believe, your expectation is infinite.

Criticisms of the Wager

Many criticisms have been leveled against Pascal's wager. Here are just a few:

1. We cannot choose our beliefs: Pascal says that the prudent option is to believe in God. But we cannot simply decide what to believe. Beliefs can't be forced. We need to feel convinced of their truth.

2. Which God? The wager argument is designed to encourage belief in the Christian God. But the same argument applies to any god who doles out infinite rewards and punishments. But clearly you can't believe in all of them.

3. Calculation is inappropriate: Beliefs acquired artificially, on the basis of self-interested calculations seem inappropriate in matters of religion. Surely, a sincere, heartfelt faith is required?

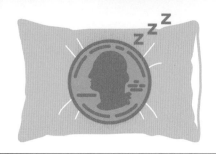

Exercise 5

You Are Sleeping Beauty

THE PROBLEM:

You are told on Sunday that you will be put to sleep that evening as part of an experiment to end Wednesday. During the experiment, you will be woken on Monday. You will soon be told that it is Monday, but before you are put to sleep again, your memory will be erased, or rather set back to what it was Sunday night before bed. You may also be woken once more on Tuesday, but (as you are told Sunday) that will depend on the toss of a fair coin. If the coin lands heads, you will be woken Monday only. If it lands tails, you will also be woken Tuesday. You have just been woken up in the midst of this experiment, but have not yet been told what day it is. Due to the memory drug, a Tuesday wakening will be indistinguishable from a Monday wakening. Your question: what degree of belief should you accord to the proposition that the coin toss came up heads?

MONTY'S METHOD:

If it's Tuesday, the coin toss must have been tails, since that is the only condition in which you are awakened on Tuesday. But if it's Monday, the coin could have come up heads or tails. Thus there remain only three open possibilities:

	Heads	Tails
Monday		
Tuesday	X	

Shaded area (marked with X) is ruled out.

Since you have no reason to believe any one of them is any more likely than any other, each possible situation deserves equal credit, and exactly one-third of your credence (degree or strength of belief). That includes the outcome that the coin lands heads. Where 1 = certain and 0=impossible (or ruled out), your credence ought to equal ⅓.

But here's another argument why you should only consider heads one-third likely. Suppose the experiment were repeated weekly over a very long period. In these trials, since the coin is fair, heads would come up just as often as tails. But for every occurrence of heads you are woken up only once, whereas each time tails is tossed you are woken up twice. In the long run, therefore, you will be woken up due to tails twice as often as you are woken due to heads. So you see, Beauty, you ought to consider the likelihood of tails to be twice as high as the likelihood of heads, which again points to a credence of tails = ⅔ and a credence of heads = ⅓. Once again, you should believe that the chances you got heads is one in three.

JUDY'S METHOD:

Nonsense! The coin is assumed to be fair. The chances that it came up heads are 50-50. So the credence or degree of belief you ought to accord to heads is ½.

Don't listen to Monty's advice. He assumes the coin was already tossed, but, despite appearances, nothing at all has been said about when the coin is to be tossed. The time of the coin toss is still up in the air!

Was it thrown on Sunday before the experiment was explained to you, or afterward but before you were put to sleep that night? Perhaps the coin toss took place while you slept, before you were just now awakened. Monty seems to have assumed this, but for all you know, the coin toss has yet to occur. Perhaps it is Monday now, and the experimenters will come here in a moment and tell you so, then reset your memory, and put you to sleep, and only then toss the coin. Can the likelihood of heads of a fair coin toss that has yet to take place really be taken as one-third, as Monty suggests? Let's get serious.

It makes no difference when the coin is tossed, only that the coin is fair. If the coin is fair, the chances that it comes up heads are ½. How can thinking now about what you already knew Sunday night (that you would only be woken on Tuesday if a fair coin toss turned up tails) reduce the likelihood of heads to ⅓ on a toss that may or may not have already taken place? Mere awakening gives you no new relevant evidence to alter this picture.

THE SOLUTION:

Let's suppose now that you are told that it is Monday. Should this new piece of information change your degree of belief in a heads result?

Both thirders (like Monty) and halfers (like Judy) think your credence in heads should now rise. Thirders think it should now rise to half; halfers will say it should rise to two thirds. Why? You do learn something in finding out it is Monday, and that changes the subjective probabilities. For instance, you now know that your memory will soon be reset to Sunday night, and that soon you will again be put to sleep. You also know that Tuesday is in the future and you are not now in that future. This means that one of the three open boxes in the table opposite (Tuesday-tails, bottom-right) is now effectively closed. You woke up knowing you might be in any one of three possibilities, now you know you might be in any one of two remaining possibilities. For this reason, the believability of heads, given that it is Monday, changes slightly.

Chapter 6

Space and Time

Space and time are abstractions, yet they make up our concrete reality. Analysis of their structure reveals a stunning array of bewildering paradoxes. Among the most fecund and beloved of philosophy, these paradoxes have also enriched physics, both ancient and recent. Often turning on the mathematics of infinity, they can serve to reveal the quizzical powers of fictional gods, who, unconstrained by the laws of physics and the finitude of earth, play an important role of illustrating and intensifying the philosophical wonderment of paradox.

Profile

Zeno of Elea

Mention the word "paradox" to anyone who's at all interested in philosophy, mathematics, or science, and the name Zeno will likely spring to mind. Zeno of Elea, to be precise (to avoid confusion with the Stoic philosopher, Zeno of Citium).

Like Eubulides (pp. 48–49), Zeno (ca. 490– ca. 430 BCE) is best known as the inventor of some ingenious paradoxes. Zeno's paradoxes, like those of Eubulides, are interesting, important, and challenging enough to have withstood the test of time, and are still hotly debated today.

In fact, Zeno's fame exceeds that of Eubulides. His paradox of Achilles and the Tortoise (pp. 128–129) is well known even to those with no special interest in philosophy (probably because it is expressed in the form of a story and has interesting characters, like one of Aesop's fables).

Zeno was the favorite pupil (and, some say, lover) of the philosopher Parmenides (ca. 520–ca. 450 BCE). They both came from the Greek colony of Elea in southern Italy.

Plato tells us that Parmenides and Zeno visited Athens around 450 BCE and became acquainted with the young Socrates. The three of them seem to have hit it off quite well, and Parmenides's philosophy is thought to have had a lasting influence on Socrates.

Not a great deal is known about Zeno's life, but legends abound regarding his death.

After returning to Elea from Athens, he is said to have become involved in a plot against Nearchus, the city's tyrant. The plot failed, and Nearchus had Zeno interrogated, tortured, and then killed.

Some accounts say that during interrogation Zeno named Nearchus's friends as co-conspirators; others say that he bit off his own tongue and spat it at the tyrant; still others say that he leaped at Nearchus and bit off his nose.

The Background to Zeno's Paradoxes
Parmenides's ideas were diametrically opposed to those of Heraclitus (pp. 46–47). Bertrand Russell neatly summarized the difference: "Heraclitus maintained that everything changes; Parmenides retorted that nothing changes."

The world, as it appears to our senses, is made up of discrete objects of varying sizes, which move around and change over time. But Parmenides considered the senses deceptive. He taught that, contrary to appearances, the universe is one thing and changeless.

According to him, the only true being is "the One": a material substance that is infinite, timeless, changeless, and indivisible. By this account, time, change, motion, divisibility, and plurality are mere illusions.

Zeno's paradoxes are designed to show that our everyday notions about time and motion, and so on cannot withstand logical scrutiny. Thus Zeno provides indirect support for Parmenides's contention that reality is an eternal, unchanging oneness.

The paradoxes use the *reductio ad absurdum* style of argument (pp. 84–85). Zeno begins by assuming that, say, time and motion exist, or that the universe contains multiple existents. Then he proceeds to draw absurd conclusions from these assumptions, thereby discrediting them.

Zeno Versus Plurality

Zeno's best-known paradoxes are directed against the concept of motion. They are discussed on pp. 128–131. In the meantime, here is another of Zeno's paradoxes: this one directed against the notions of plurality and size.

Begin with the assumption that the universe contains objects of various sizes. If an object has a size then it must have parts. Therefore it is not a single object, but rather a conglomeration of smaller ones. A true, individual object must have no size. But an object with no size is nothing at all. And any conglomeration of no-sized objects will itself have no size, and is therefore also nothing.

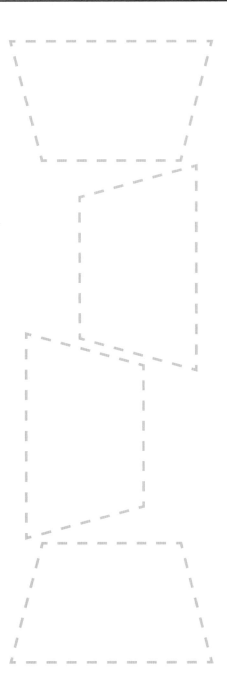

Achilles and the Tortoise

Zeno's most celebrated paradoxes concern motion. Sadly, almost none of Zeno's writing survives intact, so our knowledge of his motion paradoxes comes to us second-hand, through the writings of Aristotle.

Achilles and the Tortoise

In this famous paradox, Zeno asks us to imagine a race between Achilles and a tortoise. Achilles is a fine athlete, whereas the tortoise is… well, a tortoise. Since Achilles is much swifter than the tortoise, he gives it a head-start. But it is a long race, and Achilles has plenty of time to catch up.

Who will win? Achilles, obviously.

Not so fast, says Zeno. If we think about it logically we will see that Achilles cannot win the race without first overtaking the tortoise. But he cannot overtake the tortoise without first catching it up. And this is something he can never do.

The argument goes like this. No matter how fast Achilles runs it will take him some amount of time to catch up with the tortoise. But during this time the tortoise will have moved to a new location farther along the racetrack.

Achilles must now catch up with the tortoise at its new location. But no matter how fast he runs this will take him some time. During this time, the tortoise will have moved to another location still farther along the racetrack. And so on, and so on, ad infinitum.

Achilles can never catch up with the tortoise, let alone pass it. Therefore he cannot win the race.

Stop and Think

Zeno's argument is subtle and ingenious. But few readers will be ready to accept it. After all, we know that speedy athletes can overtake slow-moving tortoises. There must be a flaw somewhere in Zeno's reasoning. The question is, where?

The paradox of Achilles and the Tortoise has been discussed by philosophers for more than two millennia. There have been many approaches to resolving it. This picturesque one derives from an article by Alan R. White, which appeared in the magazine, *Mind*, in 1963.

Achilles at the Shooting Gallery

The shade (in other words ghost or phantom) of Achilles decides to try his luck at a shooting gallery. The shade of Zeno offers him some advice. "To hit the target," he says, "you must aim at its present position."

Achilles takes Zeno's advice. He picks up a gun, takes accurate aim, and pulls the trigger. But by the time the bullet reaches its mark the target has moved on, and the shot misses.

Achilles tries again: this time with a more responsive gun and faster bullets. But to no avail. His bullets still fall slightly left of the targets, which are moving to the right.

Luckily for Achilles, the shade of Socrates appears. "You'll never hit the center of a moving target by aiming at its present position," he says. "You must aim slightly to the right: to the place where the target will be when the bullet arrives." Achilles takes Socrates's advice and hits the next target dead-center.

What is the point of the story of Achilles at the shooting gallery? Does it help to pinpoint the flaw in Zeno's argument?

Alan R. White's point is that the paradox of Achilles and the Tortoise misleads us in the same way that Zeno misleads Achilles at the shooting gallery.

Achilles cannot hit a moving target by aiming at the point where it is, but only by aiming at the point where it will be. Similarly, Achilles can never catch the tortoise by running to its present location. But he can easily catch it by running to meet it at a future location.

White says: "Zeno has not proved that the tortoise cannot be caught; what he has undoubtedly proved is that he cannot be caught by any series of gap closures."

This all sounds perfectly sensible. It seems that Achilles can overtake the tortoise simply by running toward a point farther along than its present position—the winning post, for example.

But here, perhaps Zeno would smile and say, "Ah, yes—the only problem is that Achilles can never reach the winning post, or indeed any other point along the racetrack." His reasons for making this startling claim are discussed on pp. 130–131.

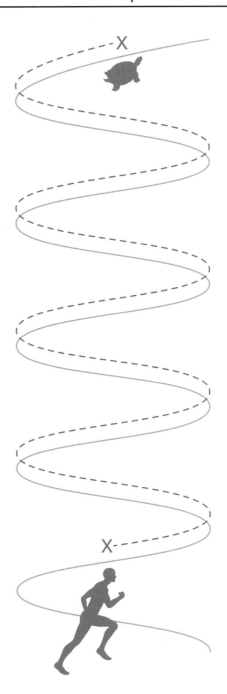

The Racecourse

Zeno's paradox of Achilles and the Tortoise (pp. 128–129) purports to show that swift-moving Achilles can never overtake a slow-moving tortoise, no matter how fast he runs and no matter how long the race. In the Racecourse Paradox (also known as the Dichotomy), Zeno goes a step further. He demonstrates that no athlete, however swift, can ever reach the end of a racecourse. Here's how:

The Racecourse Paradox

In order for an athlete to run the length of a racecourse, he must first reach the halfway point. This leaves him half of the original distance left to cover.

In order to run this remaining distance, he must first run half of it. This leaves him with a quarter of the racecourse left to cover.

In order to run this remaining quarter of the racecourse, he must first run half of it, which leaves him with one eighth of the racecourse still to cover.

But this process goes on forever. The athlete can complete the race only by running an infinite number of ever-diminishing distances. But this is impossible, since no one can cover an infinite number of distances in a finite time. Therefore the athlete cannot reach the end of the racecourse.

Precisely the same reasoning applies to anyone or anything traveling anywhere. Achilles can never reach the end of the racecourse, and neither can the tortoise. Neither you nor I can so much as cross from one side of a room to the other. Indeed, nothing can travel anywhere, since moving even the merest inch requires first traveling ½ in, then ¼ in, then ⅛ in, and so on.

Refuting Zeno

Zeno designed the Racecourse Paradox to lend indirect support to Parmenides's claim that, contrary to appearances, nothing moves or changes (see pp. 126–127). Zeno wants to convince us that the concept of motion is logically flawed, and must therefore be abandoned.

For the best part of 2,500 years, philosophers, mathematicians, and scientists have pitted their wits against Zeno. Rather than accepting his bizarre conclusions, they have sought to refute his argument. The following mathematical response is considered by many to deliver a knock-out blow.

Summing the Infinite Series

Assume, for the sake of simplicity, that the racecourse is one mile long. Thus the athlete must cover $\frac{1}{2}$ mile; then $\frac{1}{4}$ mile; then $\frac{1}{8}$ mile; then $\frac{1}{16}$ mile; and so on. Assume also that he runs at a (very impressive) speed of 1 mile per minute. In this case, he will cover the ever-diminishing distances in successively shorter times: $\frac{1}{2}$ minute, $\frac{1}{4}$ minute, $\frac{1}{8}$ minute, $\frac{1}{16}$ minute, etc.

The total time taken to complete the course is therefore:
$\frac{1}{2} + \frac{1}{4} + \frac{1}{8} + \frac{1}{16} + \frac{1}{32} + \frac{1}{64} + \ldots + \frac{1}{2^n} + \frac{1}{2^{n+1}} + \ldots$ minutes.

Zeno seems to think that summing an infinite number of fractions like this must yield an infinite sum. But mathematicians now know that this is not so. As successive terms in this particular series are added, the sum converges (gets closer and closer) to the limit of 1.

The runner is thus able to travel an infinite number of distances in a finite time, because each successive interval is shorter than the last, and the sum of those intervals converges to a finite limit.

Author's Note

Although the math appears flawless, there's something about this refutation of Zeno's paradox that doesn't quite scratch my itch.

Somehow, in reaching the winning post, the athlete must succeed in completing an infinite number of journeys. Admittedly, he completes them ever more quickly, and the sum of the time-intervals converges to a finite limit.

But even so, I find there's still something disquieting about the notion of completing an infinite number of journeys. Which leads us nicely to: supertasks.

Supertasks

Is it possible for someone (or something) to complete an infinite series of tasks in a finite amount of time? At first hearing, this may sound like a ridiculous question. After all, whoever even suggested that such a thing might be possible?

But, in fact, the question has a very real bearing on the Racecourse Paradox. Here's why. In order to reach the winning post, it seems that Zeno's athlete must do this very thing. He must complete an infinite number of journeys in a finite time. That is, he must complete what philosophers term a *supertask*.

The English philosopher James F. Thomson devised the following paradox, which may help to shed some light (pun intended) on the subject.

Thomson's Lamp

Imagine an electric lamp with a push-button switch. The first press of the button turns the lamp on; the second press turns it off; the third press turns it back on again; and so on; and so on.

Now imagine that for a period of one minute the button is pressed repeatedly at vanishingly small time-intervals: ½ minute, ¼ minute, ⅛ minute, ¹⁄₁₆ minute, and so on. At the end of the minute, the lamp will have been switched on and off an infinite number of times. It will have completed a supertask.

Now the question arises, is the lamp's final state on or off?

Thomson claims that the lamp cannot be on, since every switching-on was followed by a switching-off. But by the same reasoning the lamp cannot be off, since every switching-off was followed by a switching-on. So the lamp is neither on nor off, although clearly it must be one or the other.

The assumption that the lamp completes a supertask leads to a contradiction. Thus Thomson claims to show, by a *reductio ad absurdum* (see pp. 84–85), that the very notion of completing a supertask is logically flawed.

Thomson Refuted

Thomson's lamp is physically unrealistic. There are compelling scientific reasons for asserting that no such lamp could exist. But, all the same, the lamp scenario seems at least logically possible. So it would appear there are logical reasons for rejecting supertasks.

However, there is a flaw in Thomson's analysis of the supertask.

The sum of successive time-intervals ($\frac{1}{2} + \frac{1}{4} + \frac{1}{8} + \frac{1}{16} + \ldots$) approaches ever closer to the limit of 1, but never quite reaches it. So the rule governing successive pressings of the button tells us precisely what state the lamp is in at any moment prior to the end of the minute, but it gives us no information at all about the lamp's status at the end of the minute.

Far from generating a contradiction regarding the lamp's status at the end of the minute, Thomson's paradox has nothing to say about it.

SOMETHING TO THINK ABOUT

Thomson's Lamp, then, doesn't seem to rule out the logical possibility of completing an infinite sequence of tasks. Even so, I continue to find supertasks disturbing. This, in turn, leaves me with an uneasy feeling about the Racecourse Paradox.

In my imagination, I picture Zeno's athlete running toward the winning post. At the same time, I picture God (I'm an agnostic, but no matter) watching his progress, and saying "beep" each time the athlete completes one of his ever-diminishing journeys: at $\frac{1}{2}$ mile, $\frac{3}{4}$ mile, $\frac{7}{8}$ mile, $\frac{15}{16}$ mile, ...

Since God is omnipotent He should have no difficulty accomplishing this task. He will, of course, have to say "beep" ever more quickly. But if God can't complete a supertask, who can?

At the end of a minute, when the athlete reaches the winning post, God will have said "beep" an infinite number of times. That thought makes me feel quite queasy—whatever the mathematicians say. How about you?

Profile

Albert Einstein

The German philosopher Arthur Schopenhauer wrote: "Talent hits a target no one else can hit; Genius hits a target no one else can see." By this or any other standard, Albert Einstein (1879–1959) was a genius. His bold and startling ideas revolutionized twentieth-century science.

Einstein's interest in physics was sparked at the age of four or five when his father showed him a magnetic compass. He was fascinated by it, and tried to imagine the mysterious force that kept the needle pointing north. This same childlike curiosity drove his later work. He saw the world as a puzzle—and relished the challenge of solving it.

Despite his extraordinary talent, Einstein did not enjoy formal schooling. He found the regimented ways and unimaginative curriculum at his Munich prep school stifling. Later, he studied for a degree at the Swiss Federal Institute of Technology in Zurich, and found the teaching methods there little more suited to his tastes.

After gaining his degree, he took up employment as a technical assistant at the patent office in Zurich. The work was very undemanding for someone of his ability, leaving him plenty of spare time in which to study physics. He received his doctor's degree from the University of Zurich in 1905.

In that same year, he published three scientific papers. Each of them had a great influence on the development of physics: an astounding achievement for anyone, but scarcely conceivable for an amateur. One of those papers described his special theory of relativity (see pp. 136–137), which gave rise to the most famous equation in the history of science: $E = mc^2$.

Einstein remained at the patent office for four more years before taking up a series of academic appointments in Zurich, Prague, and Berlin. In 1915 he presented his general theory of relativity, which extended the special theory to take account of gravitational effects on space and time (see pp. 138–141).

One of the predictions of general relativity was that light beams would bend when traveling close to the sun. This prediction was confirmed by astronomers during the total solar eclipse of 1919. Newspaper headlines across the globe announced the triumph of Einstein's theory, and catapulted him to international stardom. In 1921 he was awarded the Nobel Prize in Physics.

When Hitler rose to power, Einstein left Germany and took up an appointment at the Institute of Advanced Study in Princeton, New Jersey. In 1939 he signed a letter to President Franklin D. Roosevelt warning that the Germans might be planning to build an atomic bomb (a weapon that utilized scientific principles Einstein himself had previously discovered).

This letter influenced the American government's decision to produce an "A" bomb themselves, though Einstein did not take part in its development. He later condemned the use of the atomic bomb against Japan, and campaigned for a ban on atomic weapons.

Throughout his career, Einstein combined his passion for physics with a keen moral sense and an active interest in politics. He used his fame as a platform to speak out against racism and bigotry, and denounced McCarthyism.

Space, Time, and Einstein

Pages 136–141 discuss some paradoxes associated with time travel. Time travel is an intriguing concept. Most of us have imagined journeying into the future to see the technological wonders that await us there; or traveling into the past to walk with dinosaurs, or listen to the Sermon on the Mount.

Of course, common sense tells us that all of this is strictly fiction. In reality, time cannot be altered or manipulated. It is an "ever-rolling stream" flowing relentlessly from past to future, sweeping along everything and everyone at the same unvarying pace. We cannot return to the past because the past no longer exists; we cannot visit the future, because the future has yet to unfold.

This is the view of time adopted by Sir Isaac Newton (1642–1727), whose scientific theories held sway among physicists for more than 200 years. In Newton's universe, time is absolute, irreversible, and unvarying. It is the same for everybody, everywhere.

But Newton was wrong. In 1905 Albert Einstein published his special theory of relativity, which demolished the Newtonian conception of time by showing that time is elastic. It can be stretched and shrunk.

A decade later, Einstein published his general theory of relativity which further eroded our commonsense view of time by showing that it can be warped, sometimes quite dramatically, by the presence of mass or energy.

The special theory of relativity shows that time travel into the future is scientifically unproblematic; and the general theory of relativity opens up the tantalizing possibility of time travel into the past.

Forward Time Travel

In 1905, Einstein replaced the concept of absolute time with relative time. He had been studying the way light moves, and could make sense of it only by subjecting our notion of time to a thorough overhaul. His special theory of relativity showed that the rate at which time passes for different observers depends upon their relative velocities.

Einstein predicted that a clock making a round trip will lose time compared with a clock remaining stationary at the starting point. The faster the clock travels, the more time it will lose. This slowing down of time by motion is known as *time dilation*.

For the effect to be noticeable, velocities approaching the speed of light are required. This is very fast indeed, since light travels at a colossal 186,000 miles per second (300,000 kilometers per second). Current spacecraft reach only a fraction of one percent of this speed.

The closer to the speed of light a clock travels, the bigger the time dilation effect becomes. A clock traveling at light-speed would grind completely to a halt. However, the special theory of relativity shows that light-speed is a limit that ordinary material bodies can never quite reach.

It is not only clocks that are affected by motion. All physical and biological processes are slowed down in precisely the same way. In fact, it is correct to say that time itself slows down.

Special relativity is a startling theory, but one that has been thoroughly verified experimentally. One of its most surprising aspects is that it provides a way of traveling into the future. This brand of time travel is illustrated by the so-called Twin Paradox.

The Twin Paradox

Imagine a pair of identical twins. If one twin remains stationary on earth while the other makes a round trip at a very high velocity, the second twin will age more slowly than the first. If she travels close enough to the speed of light she will be able to return to earth many generations later, having aged very little herself.

This brand of time travel is uncontroversial. True, it would require enormous advances in technology. But, in essence, a time machine capable of traveling into the future is nothing more than a spacecraft able to travel close to the speed of light.

It should be noted that the Twin Paradox is a paradox only in the weak sense that it runs counter to common sense. The notion that one member of a pair of twins can be considerably older than the other strikes us as absurd. But there is no logical contradiction or scientific impossibility involved. We just have to accept that the universe is a much stranger place than we ordinarily take it to be.

A Cautionary Tale ...

I used to teach in an elementary school. One day I happened to mention to a colleague that time passes differently for different observers depending upon their relative velocities. (Don't ask me how that came up in conversation!)

I'll never forget the look of pity he gave me. It brought to mind the words spoken by Festus to St. Paul: "Thou art beside thyself; much learning doth make thee mad."

I began to explain that time dilation effects are predicted by Einstein's special theory of relativity, and have been thoroughly verified experimentally. But to no avail. No amount of "science" could convince him that his commonsense intuitions were wrong.

But common sense can be a very unreliable guide to unfamiliar situations. The philosopher John Locke (1632–1704) gives the telling example of an Indian prince who, having lived always in a warm climate, refused to believe in the existence of ice.

In a similar way, my colleague's ideas about time were limited by the fact that he inhabits a part of the universe in which large objects move very much more slowly than light. Time dilation effects fall outside his everyday experience, and therefore struck him as absurd.

The moral of this cautionary tale? Bertrand Russell put it well: "Whoever wishes to become a philosopher must learn not to be frightened by absurdities."

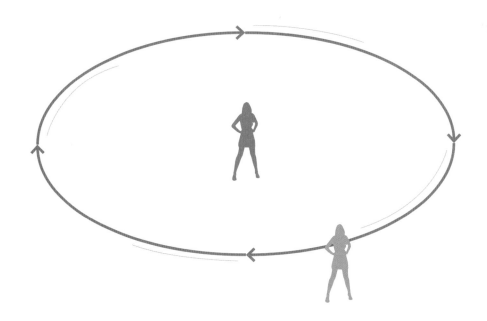

Backward Time Travel: Part 1

We normally think of space and time as entirely separate entities. But in Einstein's universe the three dimensions of space and one dimension of time are combined together into a four-dimensional continuum known as space-time. All events—past, present, and future—can be located by four space-time coordinates that specify when and where they take place.

Rather than thinking of time as flowing from past to future, most physicists accept the idea that events simply exist in space-time. This conception of time is known as the *block universe*. The terms "past," "present," and "future" have no special significance in the block universe. All events, whatever their location in space-time, are considered equally real.

In a letter to a friend, Einstein once wrote: "We physicists believe the separation between past, present, and future is only an illusion, although a convincing one."

By this reckoning, the past and the future exist just as surely as the present. They are both "out there." Special relativity already provides us with a method of traveling to the future. Events from the past can also be visited, provided that we can find a way to navigate through spacetime toward them. This is where general relativity comes in.

In his general theory of relativity, Einstein extended special relativity to take account of gravitational effects. Central to the theory is the idea that gravity is the result of mass and energy warping space-time.

Very dense matter can warp space and time quite dramatically. Theoretically it is possible for space-time to become

sufficiently warped to lead to the existence of "closed time-like curves" (CTCs). These are pathways through space-time that loop back on themselves. CTCs are potentially corridors to the past. If an astronaut could safely navigate one, he could travel into the past and participate in events there.

In 1949, the Austrian logician Kurt Gödel offered solutions to Einstein's field equations of gravitation that allow such journeys into the past. However, his solutions apply only to a rotating, non-expanding universe. Our universe is expanding and does not appear to rotate. Nonetheless, Gödel's calculations demonstrated that unrestricted time travel is possible at least in principle, and led to the search for other situations in which time travel to the past might be possible.

Some physicists have suggested that a rotating black hole could distort space-time sufficiently to produce CTCs. An astronaut plunging into one could, in theory, emerge from it at a time earlier than that at which he entered, but only if it rotated sufficiently quickly to allow him to escape from it. Unfortunately, it seems unlikely that any naturally occurring black holes rotate at the required rate.

In the 1970s, physicist Frank Tipler calculated that a rapidly rotating, super-

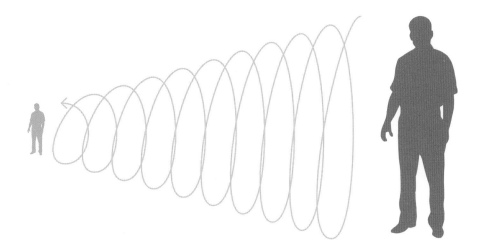

dense cylinder could create a gravitational field capable of distorting space-time enough to allow time travel. A long, thin cylinder with a mass of ten suns, spinning at a few billion revolutions per minute, would do the job. The creation of a "time machine" of this type is, however, physically unrealistic.

Kip Thorne of the California Institute of Technology has argued that by manipulating the two ends of a wormhole (a type of shortcut through space-time) one could form a CTC. Creating a traversable wormhole suitable for traveling through time is fraught with scientific and technological difficulties, which would require the resources of a civilization far in advance of our own. But this is not to say that it is impossible.

Perhaps time travel into the past is just a pipe dream. Scientists may uncover a physical law that forbids it. Or the technical challenges may prove insurmountable. But for the moment it remains a tantalizing possibility.

TO THINK ABOUT...

If backward time travel is ever to become a reality, where are all the time-tourists? Surely the pivotal moments in history will attract massive influxes of sightseers from the future. And surely someone from the future will want to intervene to prevent the rise to power of Adolf Hitler, or the crucifixion of Christ.

Backward Time Travel: Part 2

No one has yet found a compelling scientific reason to reject time travel. But there may be some logical objections to it, since the possibility of traveling to the past throws up some worrying paradoxes.

The Grandfather Paradox

If backward time travel is possible then what is to stop someone from going back to a time before the birth of his father in order to kill his grandfather? On the face of it, nothing. However, if he succeeds he will prevent the birth of his father and thus guarantee his own non-existence, which is clearly absurd.

The Knowledge Paradox

Backward time travel seems to allow scenarios such as the following.

A young man is given a book by an old man. The book contains information about how to build a time machine, which the young man then sets about building. Years later, as an old man, he travels back in time and gives the very same book to his younger self.

This is a very weird state of affairs. The book is neither created nor destroyed. Furthermore, the knowledge contained in the book comes from nowhere, without anybody expending any effort to acquire it.

Tackling the Grandfather Paradox

Some scientists, anxious to avoid grandfather-type paradoxes, have opted to rule out the possibility of time travel by invoking some kind of physical law that forbids it. For example, Stephen Hawking

has proposed a chronology protection conjecture, which says that the laws of physics will always conspire to prevent backward time travel.

Other scientists believe that the paradoxes can be resolved. One school of thought maintains that time travelers' actions will be subject to unusual constraints. Put simply: you can visit the past but you can't change it.

For example, imagine you travel back to when your grandfather was young with the intention of shooting and killing him. You will find that circumstances conspire against you. Maybe the gun's trigger-mechanism will jam. Or perhaps you will have a sudden change of heart. Maybe you will succeed only in wounding him. In which case, he may end up in hospital, being cared for by a nurse who bears an uncanny resemblance to your grandmother…

Another school of thought maintains that the many-universes interpretation of quantum theory holds the key to resolving time-travel paradoxes. According to this theory, physical reality consists of a collection of parallel universes. Some scientists claim that in the presence of closed time-like curves these normally parallel universes link up in an unusual way. A time traveler journeying backward through time along a CTC emerges in a different universe from the one he left. This means that he can exit a universe where his grandfather lives to a ripe old age, but enter an alternate universe in which his grandfather dies young.

CHALLENGING: TACKLING THE KNOWLEDGE PARADOX

There are, then, a number of approaches to dealing with the Grandfather Paradox. But what about the Knowledge Paradox? Can you think of any ways of tackling it—apart from rejecting time travel out of hand?

SOME POSSIBLE SOLUTIONS

My first thought is this: although backward time travel seems to allow Knowledge Paradox scenarios, this isn't to say that it entails them. So perhaps we can simply ignore the problem.

My second thought is that the many-universes interpretation of quantum mechanics may, once again, come to the rescue.

For example, a time-traveler could, by normal scientific processes, discover how to build a time machine. He could write down this knowledge in a book, build the machine, and then travel back in time to present the book to his younger self. Having successfully navigated a CTC, he would emerge in a different universe from the one he left.

In this way, he could pass on the knowledge in the book to his younger self without engendering a paradox. The book, and the knowledge contained in it, would be the result of genuine creative effort—albeit in another universe.

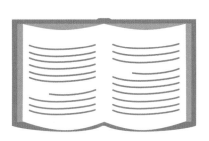

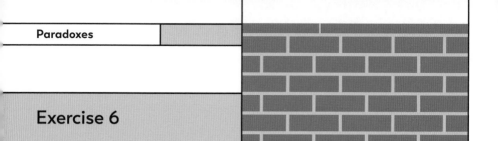

Exercise 6

Paradox of the Gods

THE PROBLEM:

A man is intent upon walking from point A to point B, a distance of just over one mile. But an infinity of gods lie in wait intending to obstruct him by erecting walls in his path should he make any progress. One god will erect a barrier to prevent him getting farther than $\frac{1}{2}$ the full distance. Another is doubly cautious, and will erect a barrier if he gets so far as $\frac{1}{4}$ of the way. A third god is twice as cautious as the second one, and will erect such a barrier to stop the man at only $\frac{1}{8}$ of the distance. In general, the nth god will erect a barrier at $\frac{1}{2^n}$ of the way to block the man's further progress.

Show that the man will never begin his journey, though no barrier need ever get built.

THE METHOD:

For ease of division, the metric system has been used in this paradox. Assume the man begins his journey, then prove a contradiction. It will follow that the man cannot begin. We'll get to the lack of need for barriers later. It will be convenient to assume that the distance between A and B is 1.024 km (=1024=2^{10} meters).

Suppose, then, that the man's first step is 1 meter (it could be any finite distance). Now 1 meter = 1.024 km/2^{10}, while 2 meters = 1.024 km/2^9. Therefore the 9th god will have erected a barrier at 1 meter before he gets there. But he won't get

there, because the 10th god, being twice as cautious as the 9th, will have already planted a barrier at 0.5 meters before the man arrives there. So the man will never get to 1 meter, as supposed; he will have been blocked already at half a meter. And even this spot he can't reach, because by the time he gets even half the way to halfway, the 11th god will have blocked him at 250 cm. This reasoning may be iterated. The 20th god will stop him before he crosses the first centimeter (1.024 km/2^{20}=0.977 cm).

To put it generally, the man cannot move any fraction, however small, of the distance from A to B, because before he gets even halfway across that fraction, some god or other will have already erected a barrier to block his earlier path. If the man can get started at all, he will already have been stopped. So clearly this man cannot even begin his journey. This is a journey of 1 kilometer that cannot begin with even the tiniest first step.

But why is it that no barrier need actually arise to prevent him? Because there can be no first barrier to arise. Note that a single divine barrier will stop any mortal in their tracks, so that more than one barrier is always redundant. We may assume, therefore, that no god will bother to set a barrier if some other god has already erected one. Thus if we can show that no first barrier can arise, it will follow that none can arise.

Assume, then, that a first barrier *could* arise. If we can derive a contradiction from this assumption, we can prove that no first barrier can arise.

Suppose the first barrier has arisen at $\frac{1}{2^m}$ of the distance from point A to point B. It will have been erected by the mth god. Since it's the first barrier, the man will be unimpeded prior to this point, and in particular, he will have faced no barrier at the half-way point between A and this first barrier. That halfway point lies at $\frac{1}{2^{m+1}}$ of the distance from journey start to finish. However, that point will already have been blocked by the $m+1^{th}$ god, who is twice as cautious as the mth god. This is a barrier before the first one, which is absurd. So there can be no first barrier. And if there is no first barrier, there can be none at all.

Now, about those gods… The gods are all capable of the sophisticated reasoning in the previous paragraphs. So the first

god is well aware it will not be necessary for him to erect the midpoint barrier, and the second god knows that a barrier at the ¼ mark will be redundant before it is necessary, and the third god can likewise see his barrier will no longer be needed as soon as it is due, etc. etc. If the nth god need not intervene to stop the man's passage, then neither need the $n+1^{th}$ god; for that god can rest assured that, before the man gets to where his barrier must be placed ($\frac{1}{2}n+1$ point of the journey), the $n+2^{th}$ god will have already acted to obstruct the man's earlier progress. Thus it's because the man can't begin his journey, that no god need act to prevent him. It seems that the mere intentions of well-coordinated gods can prevent the actions of a mortal being, even if they remain wholly unfulfilled.

And there is this other difficulty: if no god acts, there is no reason why the man can't begin his journey, and once begun, no reason he can't bring it to an end.

THE SOLUTION:

Unhappy with this result? Take solace by reflecting on the innumerable preposterous missing assumptions that go into creating this illusion of paradox. We must stipulate that, if the opportunity arises, each god can execute his or her intentions in the time available. But each in effect has only half the time as his predecessor to construct the barrier, and thus needs to be twice as efficient. Thus no finite duration can be required to build a divine barrier, and barrier construction is effectively instantaneous, as well as instantaneously known to all the gods. Mighty indeed these gods, whose very impossibility is a precondition of this hoax of a paradox.

Chapter 7

Impossibilities

By rights, nothing in this chapter should exist. But a chapter on impossibilities is a necessity in a book on paradoxes. We begin by looking at pretend impossibilities, illusory paradoxes that are readily resolved by careful clarity. We next look at genuine impossible objects, or rather drawings of them, then pay attention to some impossible intentions. We end by considering a mathematical necessity so strange it seems it must be impossible.

The Euthyphro Dilemma

Does God will what is right because it is good and just, or is the nature of goodness determined by the fact that God wills it? This has become known as the Euthyphro Dilemma, after the Platonic dialogue in which it first appears. (Plato actually discusses the quality of "piety" in relation to "the gods," but the issue is the same—here I've used a variation of the dilemma set forth by the German philosopher Leibniz to broaden and simplify the discussion.) What makes this question paradoxical is that both options seem to present a problem for the traditional conception of God.

On the one hand, if God wills the good simply because it is good, then it seems that goodness is a quality separate from God, and something that He is therefore himself subject to. Such a being would not, arguably, be the omnipotent (all-powerful) being of traditional theology, as goodness would seem to represent an external standard that places a limitation upon His freedom of will.

Should You Trust God?

On the other hand, however, if God decides what goodness is (what is termed *Divine Command Theory*), then His decision seems arbitrary, for could He not theoretically have chosen a different quality to promote, such as selfishness, evil, or injustice? For instance, in the novels and stories of H. P. Lovecraft, the writer imagines a race of malevolent deities he calls The Great Old Ones. A worshipper who took the nature of such beings as the basis for morality would therefore be committed to all sorts of acts that would traditionally be considered "bad" or "evil," but performance of which in their eyes would be the epitome of virtue.

Goodness Inseparable from God?

Of course, there is an easy way out of the paradox, which is atheism. As with the question of whether God can create a stone that is too heavy for Him to lift, the paradox may be simply cited as one further reason why such a being cannot logically exist. That said, there have been various theological attempts to resolve it. Most of these come down on one or the other side of the debate, but a few attempt to dismiss the dilemma altogether as a misunderstanding of the divine nature and thus a pseudo-problem. For instance, medieval theologian St. Thomas Aquinas argued that we can't abstract "goodness" from God's nature, setting it apart as a distinct moral standard, but must consider it as an inseparable part of His own nature. Furthermore, we should not ask whether God might "choose" some other quality over goodness any more than we might ask Him to do something not as well as He could, for God's goodness is simply a sign of the perfection of His nature—as a rosy complexion is a sign of health, perhaps— and not a deliberate choice that He makes.

The Nature of Goodness

Though not a precise parallel, the dilemma also has a secular equivalent, for moral philosophy faces a similar question in relation to the nature of goodness. For instance, classical utilitarianism defines correct moral action as that which promotes the greatest happiness of the greatest number. As such, as noted elsewhere in this book, this may occasionally result in actions that go against our traditional notions of morality. Such problems led the philosopher G. E. Moore to conclude that goodness was essentially a non-natural property: in other words, we can't say that "good = pleasure" because we can always ask whether choosing pleasure (or whatever natural property we substitute) is always "good." And in this controversy we hear perhaps a partial echo of Plato's dilemma: are certain actions right because they make us happy, or are we happy because we do the right thing?

MORAL RELATIVISM

Of course, we don't really need to ask whether God *might* have created a different moral system, because now and throughout history, cultures have adopted a diverse range of values and beliefs.

How should we respond to that fact? A hardline religious perspective might view only a narrow selection of these values as "correct," and the remainder to be mistaken or degenerate.

Alternatively, a more tolerant, perhaps secular approach might adopt a degree of *moral relativism*, arguing that—to some degree—different social practices and values are permissible, because there *is* no single divinely created set of moral values on which "correct" moral behavior must be based.

However, what is perhaps most remarkable is the extent to which, across these diverse cultures and times, moral systems *agree* on many things—whether due to divine causes, I leave you to decide.

Descartes's Ghost

Descartes was a divided person. On the one hand, he was a scientific pioneer, keen to open up the natural and physical world to rational investigation and enquiry. But he was also devoutly religious, concerned to protect religious belief from the creeping threat of atheism. Despite these seemingly opposite convictions, Descartes believed that if we could clearly distinguish between mind and matter, and show that both were separate, independent, and distinct, then religion and science could happily coexist.

Descartes was a dualist, believing that everything that exists (aside from God) is made up of either matter or mind. Matter is everything that we can see, taste, touch, feel, etc.—everything that physically exists. As such, this material stuff is measurable and quantifiable, occupies space, has volume and weight, size and dimension, and is divisible. In contrast, the immaterial or incorporeal stuff that constitutes mind possesses no physical properties at all: you can't weigh or measure it; it doesn't exist in one particular place; has no size or shape; and you certainly can't cut it up into bits.

Conscious Beings

As we saw earlier, Descartes concluded that it's impossible for me to doubt my own existence (the *cogito* argument). However, he continued, I may doubt the existence of my body, for whether I'm sitting, standing, running, eating, or performing any other activity that involves action or feeling, I may be dreaming, or cosmically deceived. However, what a conscious being cannot doubt is that they are thinking (note: Descartes defined "thought" quite broadly here, to include sensations and perceptions). As a result,

all we can really be certain of is that we are conscious beings, and that our essential activity is thought.

Mind and Body Are Separate

For argument's sake, let's assume he's right, and that mind and body are completely separate and distinct substances. How, then, do they interact? It seems obvious that the mind affects the body, and vice versa: I hit my knee and I feel pain; I decide to open a door, and my hand reaches for the handle. But, as Descartes's contemporaries were quick to point out, how can immaterial and material things affect each other?

How Does Thought Translate into Action?

Descartes provides two main solutions, but neither seems very convincing. First, he suggested that the soul might send commands and receive impressions through the pineal gland (situated in the limbic system in the mid brain). But aside from seeming like a curiously random guess (why there specifically?), the solution simply restates the question: how do physical sensations translate into immaterial impressions within the pineal gland? His other answer suffers from similar deficiencies. Perhaps, he said, mind does not interact via one spot, but is rather spread throughout the body, intermingled with some type of physical spirit-like force that allows it thereby to move the nerves and muscles. But, once again, how? So, it would seem, paradoxically, that in order for mind and body to be completely separate substances, they would also need to have physical/mental aspects with which to interact. There are, however, other possible solutions. The simplest, of course, is to reject dualism, and to admit that the mind is simply the brain. There is no separate "soul stuff." We are purely physical beings. And this is the position that most modern philosophers now propose, though it is in itself not one without difficulties. For while there is no problem as to how the various neurons and synapses interact with one another, there remains the deeply puzzling question of how specific arrangements of physical stuff result in the varied and wonderful thoughts, feelings, and impressions that constitute our subjective mental life. The debate rumbles on.

ZOMBIES

The opposite of Descartes's ghost is perhaps the philosophical zombie. While most philosophers now reject Descartes's notion of immaterial substance, there remains the problem of how some forms of matter are conscious, and others not. Why do I think, feel, taste, see, etc., and that rock (or car, or waterfall) does not?

Some philosophers argue that consciousness is merely the result of a complex arrangement of matter, but others reject this as not adequately explaining anything: if we're no more than physical parts, then wouldn't it be possible for a machine (or "zombie") to behave and act as humans do, without possessing any of the corresponding "internal" sensations and perceptions?

If such a being is even logically conceivable, then this suggests that consciousness is more than behavior or physical organization—so, perhaps, Descartes was not completely wrong.

However, of course, there's another possibility: we're all really zombies—and we just don't know it.

Something from Nothing

Whether scientific, religious, or mythical, most cultures give some sort of account of how the universe began. This may involve the imposition of order upon chaos by some divine force (or forces), the creation of the universe by the dismemberment of some pre-existing primordial being, or even such a being's spontaneous act of creation out of nothing (*ex nihilo*). And so, although these accounts vary somewhat, and a minority propose that the universe has always been around, most tend to agree that there was a point when everything got going.

As a result, religiously minded philosophers have long pointed to the fact of the universe's existence as proof that *something* must have created it (what has become known as the Cosmological Argument): but that something cannot itself have been created—the buck must stop somewhere. Therefore, there must be a *first cause*, something that has always existed or else was responsible for creating itself (*a causa sui*). And so, from Parmenides, through Plato, Aristotle, and Thomas Aquinas, philosophers have presumed that "nothing can come from nothing," and that creation *ex nihilo* is impossible.

What Came First: God or the Universe?

But if it seems unthinkable that something can simply pop into existence, then it must be conceded that the opposite is equally problematic. As David Hume argued, simply because individual events must have causes, this does not mean the universe itself must also have a cause: what is true of the parts is not necessarily true of the whole, and vice versa. The fact that your scalp is hairy does not mean that your whole body is hairy.

More fundamentally, however, the cosmological argument would seem to involve a chicken-and-egg-type paradox: if every effect must have a cause, then what about the first cause itself? Who created God? To say, as I suggested earlier, that "the buck must stop somewhere" would seem to be a case of special pleading: every effect must have a cause, apart from the first cause! And why? Because otherwise things would simply go on forever. But why is that a problem? There would seem to be no logical reason to choose between either a finite or an infinite universe (a point that Kant made—which we'll return to later).

The Big Bang

When science eventually weighed in on the matter, with the discovery of the continuing expansion of the universe by astronomer Edwin Hubble in 1929, it concluded that the universe began some 13.7 billion years ago with a massive explosion—what's now known as the Big Bang. The force of this event, and the resulting expansion it caused, as Hubble discovered, means that galaxies are still moving away from each other—in fact, as subsequent scientists have revealed, they are doing so at an increasing rate.

But, as rationally justifiable as this explanation may appear, it would also seem to leave us with a very similar problem to that faced by religious, mythical, and philosophical accounts. For here, too, we can ask, "What caused the Big Bang?" or "What came before it?" This may be scientifically annoying, but it is a legitimate question. Let's say that the Big Bang was the necessary working out of physical laws—that, given the high temperature and infinite density of the initial state of the universe (what's termed a gravitational singularity), something had to give! Even if this is true, it still seems puzzling as to why that initial state should exist, or how those laws came into existence. So, whether scientific, religious, or mythical, accounts of how the universe began seem fraught with paradox.

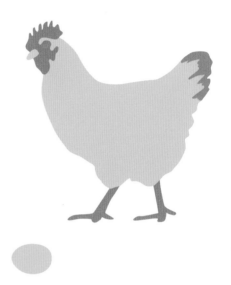

COSMIC UNCERTAINTY

As noted earlier in the book, David Hume's contribution to our understanding of the limits of scientific knowledge has been immense. It's no surprise, then, to find his name cropping up here regarding the question of the cause behind the universe.

Hume's general point is that most scientific knowledge is based on experience, and as such is not only subject potentially to change, but uncertainty: even if we could be certain that *something* created the universe, it would be almost impossible to say what exactly that thing was (one god, many gods, an impersonal cosmic force), let alone the nature of that being.

The problem here lies in arguing from effect (the universe) back to cause (the—well, the whatever!). But the same applies the other way: even if it seems clear that the universe expanded from a single point (the Big Bang), it's impossible to say with certainty what caused that.

Laplace's Demon

A great admirer of Sir Isaac Newton, and equally confident that all the laws that govern the universe would one day be laid bare, the nineteenth-century French scientist Pierre-Simon Laplace dreamed of perfect knowledge. If we reached a point where all physical laws were known to us, then, he surmised, it would be possible to predict any future outcome in advance, to know what was happening anywhere in the universe, or even perhaps to trace back events in order to ascertain what had happened in the past. All that's needed is enough data. And so, were an all-powerful, God-like intellect able to know the whole state of the universe at any one time, it could know every conceivable thing there was to know.

Laplace's Demon, as it's commonly now known, is of course hypothetical—a thought experiment, intended to show that, given time, nothing is in principle beyond the scope of the scientific mind. However, even hypothetically, there's a problem. Aside from the question of whether such a being—or even perhaps a similarly powerful computer—could exist, and even if such laws were absolutely deterministic (and we could ignore the pesky problem of quantum uncertainty . . .), we could still never with any certainty predict anything.

Chaos Theory

The reason for this is suggested by Chaos Theory, the most commonly used illustration of which is weather forecasting. Meteorology is much more accurate than it used to be, and getting better all the time. Powerful, high-speed computers help predict weather patterns both with greater accuracy and further into the future. However, despite the advances in technology and mathematical modeling techniques, things still occasionally go wrong. Why is this? It's not our knowledge of the physics involved that's the problem, as that hasn't really changed much since Newton's day; nor is it the existence of any inherent limitations regarding either computers or human reason itself. The issue is simply data.

To use the well-worn example, a butterfly flaps its wings in Rio de Janeiro, say, and later on there is a storm in Moscow. It's not that the Brazilian butterfly *causes* the Russian storm, as such, but rather that its unmeasurable "intervention" sways the final outcome.

Such an inconsequential event may not seem worth factoring into the meteorologist's calculations, but Chaos Theory argues that the impact of even such a small occurrence could ultimately radically shift the outcome—cause a storm or a hurricane—because the initial state of a system may have a disproportionate effect on that outcome. This is therefore known as the Butterfly Effect. In other words, mighty oaks from tiny acorns grow (and then are blown over in the storm). Or, as pointed out by Jeff Goldblum's character in the film *Jurassic Park*, despite the park creators' absolute certainty that they have created a system that stops their dinosaurs breeding, "nature finds a way." No system is foolproof, because it can't account for everything, and the tiniest thing can later have an unanticipated but massive effect.

Never Enough Data

Is Laplace's dream of absolute knowledge therefore paradoxical? Can there be things that can never be known even to an infinitely powerful intellect? We might hope for advances in data collection, or even theoretical physics, but the real problem here isn't that Laplace's all-powerful intellect/computer couldn't calculate the outcome of the wing-flap; it's that it could never acquire sufficient data with which to do so, because the potential influences are infinitely small. In other words, why stop at butterflies? Or gnats? Or single air particles? Or atoms? And when we get down to subatomic particles, there is a whole different problem ...

THE PROBLEM OF PREDICTION

There's another potential paradox related to Laplace's project. Let's say that at some distant point in the future someone realizes Laplace's dream by inventing an all-powerful computer that can predict everything. "Great!" you think. "Now we can stop all those terrible murders before they happen!" (You obviously work in law enforcement, for the purposes of this scenario.)

So, off you go to catch your predictable criminal. But as you're on the way, you realize something:

if you succeed in stopping the murder, then it actually means the machine is wrong—the crime wasn't committed (and the criminal, perhaps, only guilty of *intended* murder?); but if the crime happens anyway (you arrive too late, or whatever), then the machine is useless.

This is similar to a problem we'll discuss later in relation to predestination and divine omniscience—and also, incidentally, the premise for Philip K. Dick's *The Minority Report*.

The Observer Paradox

As considered earlier, the thought experiment proposed by Erwin Schrödinger (Schrödinger's Cat) illustrates just how weird the universe is at the quantum level. Until we open the box, the laws of physics cannot tell us whether the cat within it is alive or dead. How deeply puzzling this is may be further suggested by the fact that Schrödinger himself proposed the idea in order to convince people that there was a problem with quantum physics: such alive-dead cat craziness cannot be the last word on the fundamental nature of the universe, surely?

What, then, governs the cat's fate? Is the universe random? Are there secret variables that we are not aware of (as Einstein once thought)? There have been many proposed solutions to the problem of quantum indeterminacy, one of which is simply to state that it is the observer that influences the outcome. By opening the box, it is you that (somehow) determines whether the cat lives or dies. If this is true—and it seems, from my layman's perspective, as plausible as any of the other proposed solutions to this craziness—then we are faced with a further paradox: not only, before we open the box, is the cat both/neither alive or dead, but it is not possible to observe something without influencing it. But, if true, this would seem to leave scientists with having to admit that the very act of observation alters the outcome of an experiment, thus rendering any sort of scientific objectivity impossible.

Can An Observer Ever Be Subjective?

The Observer Paradox, as it's been termed, may apply at various levels. Fortunately, quantum indeterminacy does not seem to apply at the "macro" level of buildings and people and cars, only (as

far as we know) at the "micro" level of subatomic particles. However, a looser, parallel phenomenon can be seen at work in other areas of human knowledge. For instance, an anthropologist investigating a remote indigenous tribe affects by his very presence the behavior of the people whose "unpolluted" culture he wishes to document. The same applies to the nature documentary filmmaker or the reality T.V. programmer. In social situations, the presence of the observer, or even the mere knowledge of being observed, may affect the behavior of the observed. Just think of the difficulty people often have in "acting naturally" when someone is watching. In a subtler way, observers also influence outcomes via their expectations and assumptions: even though the camera is hidden, someone made a decision to point it one way instead of another, to focus on *this* rather than *that*, and the behavior is interpreted in the light of the observer's own values; the scientist tests for a hypothesis, trying to prove (or disprove) a set of narrow possibilities, while others go unconsidered. The Observer Paradox is therefore really just an aspect of the larger problem of objectivity. In fact, the history

MANY WORLDS

Quantum indeterminacy remains a mystifying problem for physicists, but the idea that the observer in fact plays some role in determining the outcome of Schrödinger's experiment (whether the cat is alive or dead) is only one proposed solution (known as the Copenhagen Interpretation, first suggested by physicists Niels Bohr and Werner Heisenberg).

Another popular alternative is the so-called Many Worlds Interpretation, proposed by physicist Hugh Everett, where instead of the observer determining which of the two possibilities is fulfilled, Everett argues that *both* are, each possible result creating its own "world." So, in one, Schrödinger's cat is alive; in another, it's dead.

This solution—my physicist friends tell me—is actually "preferable," because, in mathematical terms, it's "neater"; but in all other ways, it would seem even more bizarre than the Copenhagen Interpretation—a factor that also perhaps explains its appeal to science-fiction writers.

of science and philosophy may be seen in terms of the struggle to identify and isolate the various obstacles to knowledge that nature (human nature in particular) puts in our way. Is objectivity, then, a forlorn hope? Are we forever paradoxically predetermined always to bring our own prejudices to the table?

On the one hand, it seems that we can never rule out the existence of the unwitting influence of the observer. On the other, we may point to the incredible practical benefits that scientific knowledge has afforded us. While it remains a theoretically fraught issue, therefore, it nonetheless seems plausible that the human race has achieved some degree of progress toward objectivity and truth—of which, the recognition of the Observer Paradox is itself (paradoxically ... ?) an example.

Kant's Antinomies

While other philosophers saw paradoxes as riddles to be solved, or indications of conceptual impossibility, Immanuel Kant argued that such contradictions highlighted questions that were beyond the capacity of human reason to comprehend. In the *Critique of Pure Reason*, he argues that there are "transcendental" questions where an equally rational and plausible case can be made for two opposing viewpoints. Regarding the problem of free will, Kant argues that it seems equally valid to assume that our conscious actions are based on free choices as it does to presume that every cause must have an effect (and that, therefore, all our actions are predetermined). Regarding the existence and nature of the universe, doesn't it seem equally hard to deny that it has always existed as to deny that it once didn't? And isn't it also equally valid to assert that the universe is infinite in size as it is to deny this?

Kant declared such problems to be examples of "antinomy"—essentially, a paradox—cases that neither reason nor experience can solve. Take the idea that every cause has an effect, and vice versa; how do we know that? Hume (who influenced Kant) argued that it is solely through experience. If a flower opens in sunlight, we form the idea that sunlight causes flowers to open. But why do we believe this? Is there some special "cause" that we identify? No: it is simply that they happen together, again and again, and the relationship becomes fixed. Logic cannot teach us about such things; only experience.

Making Sense of Experiences

Kant took Hume's point and suggested a deeper possibility: what if such assumptions (e.g. that every effect has a cause) are not something we learn, but preconditions of experience itself? In other words, it's something we need to assume in order to make sense of experience—a world without these concepts wouldn't even be comprehensible. And because of this, certain transcendental questions cannot be settled by either reason *or* experience. For instance, to take another of Kant's examples, let's consider the question of atomism—the idea that the

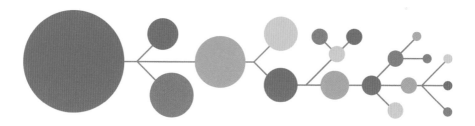

universe consists of tiny, irreducible particles of matter (atoms). Now, as twentieth-century physicists have shown, the atom may be split, revealing a whole plethora of smaller subatomic particles. It boggles the mind to think that this splitting might go on forever, yet any ultimate particle we discovered would also, presumably, have size and dimensions, and could therefore presumably have "parts." So what's the solution? Kant argues that both assumptions—that the world is made up of simple elements, and that all things are complex—are based on experience. "Simple" and "complex" are ideas we form from experience, and cannot therefore be used to reason about the nature of experience as a whole.

Kant's Transcendental Method

So, should we simply give up trying to answer such questions? Not necessarily. For instance, although Kant criticizes and rejects many of the traditional arguments for the existence of God, he does present an alternative argument: for moral behavior to be considered rational, there must be justice (otherwise, being moral would be irrational); justice is not always done on earth, therefore it must be enforced in heaven after death, by God. I'm simplifying greatly here, but it reveals the difference in Kant's approach (called the transcendental method): instead of asking whether God exists, he asks what would need to be the case in order for morality to be rational. It's an indirect form of argument, thus avoiding the sort of paradox (antinomy) that besets traditional approaches.

THE FLY IN THE BOTTLE

The idea that there may be limits to human thought—what it's possible to conceive of or talk about—has interested other philosophers besides Kant, the most notable being Wittgenstein.

As we saw earlier, Wittgenstein argued that language and thought were closely related, and both were shaped by human behavior and culture. As he famously put it, "The limits of my language mean the limits of my world" and so, "what we cannot think we cannot say either."

Consequently, paradoxes and other forms of philosophical conundrum reveal those limits—the things about which it's impossible to think or talk. From this point of view, many traditional philosophical controversies are revealed as *pseudo* problems, mere confusions resulting from our inability to recognize the limits of thought.

In understanding these limits, we therefore escape our puzzlement much like a fly that finally finds its way out of the bottle in which it has been trapped.

Varieties of Impossibility

To be impossible is almost a contradiction in terms. If something is impossible, it cannot be. So how can we speak of being impossible at all? Impossibility is rather a form of necessary non-being. The impossible does not exist because it cannot exist. The impossible is a species of nothing. And if the impossible is nothing, surely nothing is impossible.

On What There Isn't

There is an old philosophical question about whether holes exist. A hole is not so much a something as a nothing—a lack, an absence, something missing. But you can count holes, which means that many exist. If many holes exist, why shouldn't one exist? If there are more holes in a piece of Swiss cheese than there are in this argument, then that means there must exist at least one extra hole in that cheese that is not in my argument. And if that hole exists, so does every other hole.

The impossible is very much like a hole. Impossibilities may literally be nothing, but they can be counted and set out in a bewildering array of varieties. One is tempted to say that impossible objects come in many shapes and sizes; the trouble is they don't "come" at all.

And yet the impossible can not only be imagined, it can be discovered. For example, in the field of physics there is the law of conservation of energy (energy cannot be created or destroyed) and the law of special relativity (it is impossible to exceed the speed of light); also, in the field of mathematics, we saw earlier that Gödel proved a complete theory of arithmetic is impossible (see p. 75).

So it is possible to discern various types of impossibility and, as we shall see, there are

innumerable species of impossible objects. Impossibility is necessarily diverse. One might almost say that many forms of the impossible are possible, and here are some.

Practically versus Inherently Impossible

A useful distinction can be made between what is practically impossible and what is inherently impossible. What is practically impossible today may be routine tomorrow, for instance if technology develops. Travel to the moon was once impossible, but ingenuity, determination, lots of money, and a competitive spirit changed that. It has, however, always been logically possible.

Our concern in this chapter is the more difficult impossibilities that are not due to practical obstacles. We are looking for the inherently impossible—that which cannot be achieved or realized in any way, and never can be.

Simple versus Composite Impossibility

Most impossibilities are made up of inherently possible parts that simply cannot be put together in the way proposed. For example, a self-contradiction is a proposition conjoined to its negation. Each is consistent by itself, but they mutually exclude each other so can't both be true. A married bachelor offends by being both unmarried, as are all possible bachelors, and yet married. Satyrs, centaurs, and sphinxes are all impossible monsters composed of possible parts. In this way composite impossibilities seem to be impossible wholes composed of possible parts.

Could there be an inherently impossible object not composed of possible parts? Or does it take at least two possibilities to be put together incorrectly in order to make an impossibility? One must wonder whether simple impossibility is even possible. But if a simple impossibility is simply impossible, that would surely prove to be the case in point. And, with that mind-bending thought, you may be relieved to read that simple impossibilities are too complex to be further considered here.

The Meaningless versus the Impossible

The attempt should be made to distinguish between the meaningless and the impossible. The meaningless (also called the nonsensical) is defined in some regions of philosophy as any claim that can be neither true nor false. The impossible, in contrast, is whatever is necessarily false.

Decide for yourself:

"Virtue is triangular."

"Breakfast is the first meal to become president."

These statements, you will no doubt agree, are not true. But would you call them false? To call them false has seemed

A QUESTION FROM WITTGENSTEIN

What time is it on the sun? Is it even possible for this question to have an answer? Can it be morning on the sun? Is it not 4:00 am on the sun once a day? If it is (merely) false that it is prior to 4:00 am on the sun, then is it not 4:00 am or later there?

to some philosophers to be giving them more credit than they deserve. These sentences commit category errors; they are too outlandish even to be called false. For instance, the first sentence applies a concept from one domain (geometry) to a concept from a totally different domain (ethics). This sentence is in fact a stock example of a meaningless or nonsensical claim (meaning it cannot be significantly said to be either true or false).

Against this pro-nonsense position it may be argued that, if the above claims were false, they would not be false by accident. Indeed, if they were false, they would be necessarily false, and so impossible. Moreover, those who try to distinguish the meaningless from the impossible in this way will find themselves uncomfortably committed to the claim that it is impossible that it should be true that virtue is triangular. The distinction itself becomes meaningless, and the nonsensical is seen as simply the impossibility of sense.

Transgressions Through Transitivity

Imagine a businesswoman who is detained on business in Boston, and misses home and family in Cleveland. Homesick, she sighs: "If I were not in Boston, I would be in Cleveland." We may assume she is speaking the truth. Now surely it would also be true for that person to affirm the following sentence: "If I were in Alaska, I would not be in Boston."

This innocuous conjunction leads by an apparently indubitable principle to an impossible conclusion. The principle, known as "transitivity," takes the form of valid argument: if the two premises are true, the conclusion must also be true. Check for yourself:

If A, then B.
If B, then C.
Therefore, if A, then C.

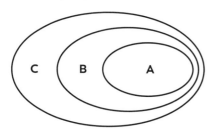

However, by an obvious process of substitution, it follows that our lonely traveler is in a position to assert: "If I were in Alaska, I would be in Cleveland." How can such geographical nonsense follow logically from true premises in a valid argument form? Could the principle of transitivity be wrong?

Well, transitivity is safe, but it is misapplied here. Transitivity assumes that the B clause (not in Boston) means the same thing in both premises; however, the vagaries of language mean it doesn't in this case. Intuitively we understand that a more complex analysis is required than simply forcing these sentences to fit the principle of transitivity.

A Biological Impossibility?
A further example of transitivity going awry can be found in the following example.

We start with an, admittedly crude, definition of a species involving the ability of two individuals belonging to it to interbreed. (This is based on biological principle, so irrelevant factors like age, opportunity, and inclination are ignored.)

Now imagine that a particular species of fish populates a lake. A catastrophic climate change dries the lake until it is no longer whole, but five smaller, separate lakes each containing roughly one fifth of the original population. Over time, each separate group evolves independently, and eventually the fish grow so different that, in some cases, interbreeding becomes biologically impossible. According to our definition this is the point at which we can say that distinct species have evolved.

Now imagine a biologist comes along and takes a number of specimens from each lake. He returns to his lab and places the different fish in the same tank. In the course of his experiments he observes the following:

Group A can interbreed with Group B.
Group B can interbreed with Group C.
Group C can interbreed with Group D.
Group D can interbreed with Group E.
Group E cannot interbreed with Group A.

We can apply transitivity to this to say that if Group A can interbreed with Group B, and Group B can interbreed with Group C, then Group A can interbreed with Group C. By applying transitivity a few more times you can reach the conclusion that Group A can interbreed with Group E—but this contradicts the observed fact that Group E cannot interbreed with Group A.

The same conundrum can be put in another way, considering groups separated not by physical barriers but by the passage of time. People of today could in principle mate with people of the previous millennium, who in turn could mate with people who lived in a millennium previous to that. Assuming transitivity, one can appear to prove that there was never a distinct species from which human beings arose.

Intuitively we know that this can't be the case, but what has gone wrong? Is our definition of a species (based on interbreeding) at fault; is the set of observed facts a biological impossibility; or is the principle of transitivity worthless?

Is the case laid out above an a priori argument against the evolution of species? Well, in a word, yes—albeit a very bad one.

In reality, what it shows is that our chosen definition is inconsistent with evolution. Despite its intuitive appeal, the definition is an abstraction with at best a local truth. Species in reality are more like individuals (like particular twigs on the evolutionary tree) rather than discrete classes.

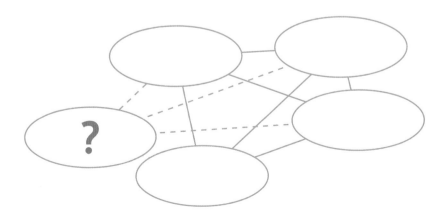

Impossible Objects

One might be excused for thinking the impossible is inconceivable. But being unable to exist is different from being unable to be thought or imagined. The impossible cannot be, but in some cases it is imaginable. Our ability to conceive the impossible may be limited, but it is greatly assisted by depictions of impossible objects. It even turns out that the impossible can be represented by a variety of means, which are startling in what they reveal about us.

Some Possible Figures

The fact that the following constructions cannot be physically created does not prevent them from making attractive images. The impossible can be depicted, and proves to be pleasantly jarring. The impossible object shown here was devised by Swedish artist Oscar Reutersvärd, a variation on his more famous tribar—also called the Penrose triangle after Lionel and Roger Penrose, who later independently rediscovered it.

Each corner in this figure is spatially coherent, but the figure as a whole is not. Each corner is shown as if from a different point of view; perspective on the whole is not unified. The result is a depiction of a structurally impossible object. No such object could exist in the three dimensions we occupy.

The distinguished scientist Richard L. Gregory has urged a distinction be made between impossible figures and impossible objects. The Penrose triangle, he insists, is an impossible figure, not an impossible object. The grounds for his distinction are that there exists after all a three-dimensional object which, when viewed from a particular perspective, looks just like a tribar.

This is demonstrated by the illustration below, which initially appears to be a Penrose triangle, but the illusion falls apart when the perspective is rotated.

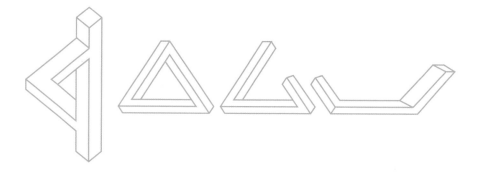

Examples of the objects depicted here have actually been built and displayed as public art, as if to defiantly affirm the existence of the impossible. Often, the illusory effect is all the more robust, because it is not a mere drawing. When you see such an object from a particular perspective, it seems to violate the very space in which it exists.

Contrary to Gregory, it ought to be said that the Penrose triangle is precisely a possible figure, not an impossible one, as its invention clearly demonstrates. The figure was invented; its possibility was discovered. What the figure represents, however, is an impossible object, an object that cannot exist in three dimensions. This is true, even though by way of trickery of perspective it can appear otherwise.

The existence of three-dimensional objects that look (from one perspective) like a tribar does not make the tribar a possible object. At most, hitherto unexpected ambiguities or alternative interpretations of the figures are introduced. What these three-dimensional objects show is that the illusion of the Penrose triangle does not depend entirely on a two-dimensional representation, but rather on perspective.

A Possible Tribar?

All the cleverness of illusion demonstrated by a tribar sculpture does not make a tribar possible. The tribar is a possible figure, but an impossible object after all. However, it is worth noting a slight caveat: While a tribar, or similarly impossible object, cannot exist in three-dimensional space, it is possible to construct animated models of them. To animate such a figure it is necessary not only to construct a

three-dimensional model on a computer, but also to alter that model as the figure rotates or the viewpoint changes. Only in this way can the illusion be retained.

The Devil's Trident

On Gregory's view, the illustration below— variously known as a poiuyt, blivet, or devil's trident—is a genuine impossible object. One ought to say on the contrary that it is only a depiction of a genuine impossible object. Cover up the top or the bottom of the image to enhance the effect.

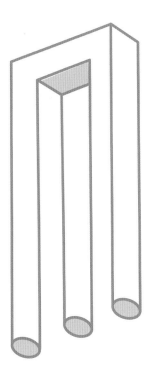

Double-Take

Perhaps you are familiar with stereoscopes, devices for viewing three-dimensional images. If the images loaded in the stereoscope represent slightly different perspectives on the same object, the two-dimensional pictures are fused by the brain to create a three-dimensional experience. This fusion is understood to be an unconscious inference based on information derived from the two retinal images. The visual experience of three dimensions is an inference.

Here's a fun impossibility: an attempt to fuse the unfusable! Just take two hollow cardboard tubes (cut an empty paper-towel roll in two) and fasten them together, as if they were binoculars. Then attach a very different image to the end of each tube. Look through them and relax your eyes.

What happens when the images are totally distinct and cannot be fused? A remarkable phenomenon known as "binocular rivalry" sets in. At first, both images jostle with each other—instead of fusing they may unstably overlap, each partially obliterating the other for a brief time. But in time one image will come to predominate, while the other disappears completely. Both eyes are still open, but only one image is seen. What has happened to the other image? Just wait a little longer, and the lost image will reappear and replace the first one, which now fades away. As you keep watching, the images slowly alternate, as if the two images were competing for your attention—and they are!

How does this happen? Well, each eye receives a totally distinct image, and both can be seen. Each of these images also activates the associated regions in the visual cortex of the brain; however,

the level of processing varies. Since the two images cannot be fused, they are like competing hypotheses about what you are looking at. When one hypothesis wins out, the processing of its image is enhanced, while the disconfirming evidence from the other image is suppressed. But it persists, making the original hypothesis shakier, until a different inference is made. The lost image now has its moment in the sun and, in this way, a competitive rivalry continues.

It Can't Be Both!

A similar rivalry occurs with bi-stable figures. These are ambiguous images that are capable of two incompatible interpretations, and below is one of the most famous—the duck–rabbit. It can't be

A PRACTICAL EXPERIMENT

Part 1: Make a cube out of stiff wire, attached at one corner to a rod. In a dark room, shine a flashlight at a wall, casting a shadow from the wire-frame cube. Rotate the cube. What do you see?

Part 2: Paint your wire cube fluorescent so it will glow in the dark. In a dark room, while it can be seen, hold it in your hands. You may experience a visual reversal despite tactile evidence to the contrary from your hands, which is a freaky experience.

both a duck and a rabbit, so your view of it alternates between one and the other and will not remain stable.

A yet simpler example of a bi-stable image is the Necker Cube—the two left-hand images at the bottom of the page—which spontaneously flits back and forth between appearing as a cube projecting into the page and one standing out of it. The image cannot be interpreted in both ways simultaneously, so alternates—which suggests representational rivalry. As a check against its own errors, the brain looks for alternative interpretations, and in this instance finds a plausible alternative, which in its turn comes to dominate.

The two images below left are bi-stable figures, which offer incompatible and competing interpretations. They are both variations on the Necker Cube, and can be seen as either projecting out from the page or cutting into it. The lower image can be seen either as a cube in linear perspective or as a truncated pyramid. By contrast, the depiction below right represents a genuinely impossible object, an object that cannot exist in real space. These illusions suggest that impossible objects exist, even though we know they can't. No coherent structural description is possible for these objects, and spatial anomalies and violations of space are perceived.

Seeing Is Disbelieving

Even four-month-old babies have been shown to be sensitive to the inconsistent relationship in the depth cues and to the structural irregularities that make the cube depicted here impossible. Meanwhile, in adults, a certain brain signal, associated with previous exposure to items in a recognition test, has been found in the case of possible objects, but not for impossible objects of comparable complexity. It is hypothesized that the brain region generating this signal is responsible for representation of the global three-dimensional structure of objects.

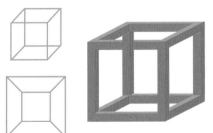

Divine Impossibilities

Suppose an omniscient being to be one who knows every truth. Now consider: "This statement is not known to be true by any being." If this statement is false, it cannot be known, even by an omniscient being. But also, if it is false that the statement is not known, it must be known, hence true. So the statement cannot be false.

Any being omniscient by the above definition would therefore know it to be true—but this contradicts the statement itself! It follows that no being knows all truths. Either there is no omniscient being, or omniscience is not the knowledge of every truth!

The Paradox of the Stone

Could God make a stone so heavy that even He could not lift it? To answer yes is to imply that there is something God could not do (lift this stone). To answer no is also to imply that there is something God could not do (create this stone). Either way there is something God cannot do. So something is impossible for God to do, and this seems to threaten the presumptive omnipotence of God. To assume God is all-powerful, together with the consideration of this stone, seems to result in a logical contradiction.

So which is it? Is the idea of omnipotence self-contradictory? Or does God's power embrace even the inherently impossible?

There are several lines of response to this paradox open to believers. A believer might accept the conclusion that God could not create such a stone, but deny that this constitutes any genuine limitation on infinite power. For instance, one might argue that, if God could create this stone, it would entail a logical contradiction; so God can't. But not being able to achieve the impossible is no skin off His nose. For, if the impossible were achievable, it would not really be impossible.

Another approach similarly concedes that God cannot create a stone He cannot lift, but uses a very different argument to show that, despite this, there is not an act that God cannot do. God's omnipotence in this regard requires only that: for any weight, God could create a stone of that weight; and for any weight, God could lift a stone of that weight.

Under these two conditions, there is no limit on God's creating or lifting of stones; yet there will not be a stone God could create but not lift. Indeed it follows from these two conditions that God can lift every stone He can create.

But this, expressed differently, says that God cannot create a stone He cannot lift. Granted, if God could create a stone He could not lift, it would be bad for His omnipotent reputation. But if He cannot create a stone He cannot lift, this is thanks to His boundless abilities, not despite them.

This neat solution suffers from the problem that "indefinitely large weights" is a radically incoherent notion. Infinite mass and gravity suffer from a physical

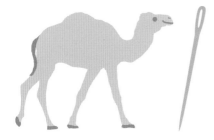

possible, then even the impossible should be possible. If nothing is impossible, again even the impossible should be possible.

The Belief in Impossibility

As author of physical laws, God may violate them at will. As author of the laws of logic, why couldn't God suspend them as well? This seems to have been the view of René Descartes:

"The truths of mathematics ... were established by God and entirely depend on Him, as much as do all the rest of His creatures. ... You will be told that if God established these truths He would be able to change them, as a king does his laws; to which it is necessary to reply that this is correct. ... In general we can be quite certain that God can do whatever we are able to understand, but not that He cannot do what we are unable to understand. For it would be presumptuous to think that our imagination extends as far as His Power," Descartes, Letter to Mersenne, April 15, 1630.

At a crucial moment, Jesus rebukes His followers whose lack of faith leaves them without the power to perform miracles: "If you have faith as small as a mustard seed, you can say to this mountain, 'Move from here to there' and it will move. Nothing will be impossible for you." (Matt. 17:20–21) So even for human beings, provided they have sufficient faith, nothing is impossible. Perhaps the true test of belief is precisely to believe the unbelievable.

incoherence God should not have to answer for. In any case, perhaps there is a more radical option for the believer.

Miracle or Contradiction?

"Jesus said 'I tell you, it is easier for a camel to go through the eye of a needle than for a rich man to enter the kingdom of God.' When the disciples heard this, they were greatly astonished and asked, 'Who then can be saved?' Jesus looked at them and said, 'With man this is impossible, but with God all things are possible.'" (Matt. 19:24–26)

Now it is physically impossible to put a camel through the eye of a needle. Of course, all that means is that it would take a miracle, a contravention of physical law, to make it happen. It would be astonishing, but it does not yet amount to a logical impossibility, or a contradiction in terms. (In fact, if it were pure geometry, it might even be a theorem; see The Pea and the Sun—pp. 168–169).

But maybe self-contradiction is simply the most extreme miracle. Perhaps the most extreme test of faith requires an attempt to believe the absurd.

So a believer may go further and ask: Is God limited by logical possibility, or does even the realm of logical self-contradiction fall within God's ambit? If all things are

The Pea and the Sun

Believe it or not, you can take a solid ball, dissect it into five disjointed pieces (one of which can be a single point), and then rearrange these by rigid motions such as translation and rotation—in other words motions that don't stretch or distort the pieces—so as to form two spheres the same size as the original one.

Alternatively, if you wish, you can dissect a ball into as few as five non-overlapping parts that can be reassembled, using rigid motions, into another ball of any volume you please. A pea-sized ball can be split and then reconstituted into a solid sphere the size of the sun.

Can such a counterintuitive idea really be true? Well, it is, albeit within the field of theoretical geometry. This very strange idea is known as the Banach–Tarski paradox, after Stefan Banach and Alfred Tarski, the two great Polish mathematicians who proved it in the 1920s.

It is known as a paradox because it is counterintuitive, but actually it is not a genuine paradox at all. Far from being necessarily false, it is necessarily true, deducible from some widely assumed mathematical principles.

Illusions of Solidity

The appearance of a paradox depends in part upon prevalent confusions regarding solidity. Even as great a philosopher as John Locke found it difficult to remove the notion of solidity from the notion of body itself. Space could be empty, he thought, but bodies in it were solid, so that where one body was no other could be at the same time. In more recent times, it has become commonplace to muse about the

conundrum propounded by the physicist James Jeans. He pointed out that since everyday solid objects like walls and tables are made up of atoms, and atoms in turn are mostly empty space, then everyday solid objects are mostly empty space. This may be subverted by mentioning the obvious opposing point that objects are not the space they occupy.

Ironically, it is only a mathematical solid that is well and truly solid. It, however, being theoretical, has no mass. The mathematical ball is a solid sphere of geometrical space. That is to say, it consists in a set of points making up a spherical region of space. Geometrical space is understood to be composed of points that may be identified by their real-number coordinates. Just as the real-number line is "made up" of points corresponding to real numbers, so three-dimensional space is represented by ordered triplets of real numbers (which give the coordinates of points in space). A ball is therefore an infinite set of points, and parts of the ball are subsets of this set of points.

The requisite subsets are discrete—in other words non-overlapping—subsets that, together, make up the original sphere. These subsets are unusual, not like the parts into which you might slice a real pea, a real baseball, or a real sun. These are not divisions of mass at all, because our mathematical ball has no mass. As scatterings of points, some of these subsets do not even have volume, which is how they can be rearranged and reassembled into a solid with a different volume. Technically, subsets of the ball involved in the Banach–Tarski dissection are said to have no measure.

How can this be shown? It is impossible to prove it here, but a rough idea of the proof can be given. First, Banach and Tarski proved their theorem by generalizing a similar result by Felix Hausdorff—a Jewish German mathematician who committed suicide in 1942 in the face of Nazi persecution. Hausdorff's theorem asserted that a sphere (that is, the surface of a mathematical ball) is equidecomposable into two copies of itself—in other words the one hollow sphere can be cut up and reordered to make two. Banach and Tarski applied this finding to a solid ball, as opposed to simply the surface, by conceiving the latter to consist of nested spheres (much like an onion is made up of several layers). This brief summary leaves the doubling of the sphere wholly unexplained, but it does give at least some hint of the approach taken.

Some Lexical Lunacy

However, the crucial idea of doubling can be suggested by considering the case of a special dictionary equidecomposable into two copies of itself. Imagine a dictionary that is simply a list of all the possible words of finite length that can be spelled with two letters, say A and B. Every finite string of As and Bs is a word in this language, and they can all be arranged in alphabetical order. All words are finite, but the number of possible words is infinite. This is a lot of words, so after the initial one-volume printing, the dictionary came out in two volumes: one containing all words starting with A, the other all words starting with B. Since all the words in each volume start with the same letter, it was considered redundant to keep repeating it. Thus all the initial As in volume one, and all the initial Bs in volume two, are left out of the second printing.

The paradoxical result is that the two volumes are now identical, all of the entries read the same, and they are also identical to the one-volume original edition. Something like this strange doubling is involved in the Hausdorff result, except in that case it involves sequences of rotations of the spheres.

Fitting a Camel Through the Eye of a Needle

If a pea-sized ball can be partitioned into discrete parts that can be rearranged to form a sun-sized ball, then it hardly seems a miracle for a camel-sized region of space to be dissected and the parts recomposed into a camel small enough to fit through the eye of a needle. A miracle involves the violation of physical law—but the Banach–Tarski Theorem is a form of mathematical law. It is not an exception to a necessity, but an expression of it.

The Toxin Paradox

THE PROBLEM:

Let us suppose a billionaire with an altruistic passion for paradox puts to you the following proposal, the terms of which the most scrupulous lawyers and experts have verified. You are to receive $1 million simply for forming an appropriate intention at midnight tonight, an intention to perform a particular act at noon tomorrow. You will not be required to perform the later act, only to intend at midnight—based on this offer alone—to commit that act tomorrow at noon. Infallible brain-scanning technology will reveal at midnight whether or not you in fact intend to act at noontime the next day.

    The act which you must intend to later perform is the ingestion of a certain toxin, which will make you very sick for 24 hours, but you will fully recover without side-effects. To get the $1 million, you must intend at midnight to ingest the toxin the following noon. Show that it is impossible to form such an intention.

THE METHOD:

It seems that it can be done, for nothing is so easy as to frame an intention, especially when the responsibility of carrying it through is so conveniently relaxed, as in this case. No one would willingly ingest this toxin, were it not for the $1 million. But acquiring $1 million is clearly preferable to avoiding the illness due to poisoning. So, intending to act is both easy and preferable, and when you add in the facts that not actually following through would bring in this case no penalty, and spare you a day of misery, the prudent person would choose to intend to take the toxin, but then later to refrain from it. This is still honest, since completion of the action is not in fact required to get the $1 million.

    But here arises a problem. To intend at midnight to take the poison next noon, requires that you not intend later to forego taking it. You cannot honestly intend to do what you also intend not to do. If you know in advance you are not going to take the poison, then you cannot intend to do so. Of course, you could pretend to intend, and merely say you are going to take the toxin later; but this won't work, as the infallible intention-detection technology will catch you in the lie.

So you can't honestly intend to do what you know you later won't. From this perspective, the unlikely billionaire's money is secure in his hands.

Various ruses may be tried to get another chance at winning that money. For instance, one could ignore the probable fact that one will not take the toxin if it is no longer necessary, and instead focus exclusively on, and try to strengthen, the resolve to swallow the poison. Think about the money that will come, not the illness that you will endure. This is a form of self-deception, deceiving oneself that something isn't true, when you know very well that it likely is. But the mere appearance to oneself of having formed an intention is not better than the mere appearance to others, and is no more likely to succeed. It is not enough to persuade yourself that you have an intention which in fact you do not; you must in fact have the intention, and not be deceived, by yourself or anyone else, into thinking you have it. The lie-detection technology is just that good.

Incidentally, there is a related paradox of self-deception. How can you deceive yourself at all, since you are privy to any plans that you might hatch to fool yourself. To deceive others, it is necessary that they not know they are being deceived. To fool yourself, it ought likewise to be impossible not to know that you are being deceived, since the ploy you are using is, after all, yours, and so not unknown to you.

Perhaps you could persuade yourself that you intend at midnight to take the toxin at next noon by making further arrangements that compel you to do so. For instance, you could sign a legal agreement requiring you to incur a $10 million cost if you do not drink the toxin at noon tomorrow, having committed to it. This gives you plenty of reliable incentive to ingest the poison in time, though again the offer itself does not strictly require you do so (only the intention to do so at midnight is needed). The billionaire's offer, however, also required that you intend to consume the toxin only on the basis of the billionaire's offer. So such additional incentives are ruled out.

THE SOLUTION:
The inventor of this paradox is Gregory Kavka. He was led to conclude that "one cannot intend whatever one wants," that "intentions are only partly volitional," and that "intentions are constrained by reasons for action." In much the same way, you cannot believe whatever we want, belief cannot be wanton, for belief is constrained in fact by reasons to believe.

Intentions, though they seem to be merely subjective and private thoughts, are not merely decisions within the mind, but aspects of the outward acts themselves. Your intention is a feature of your act, which takes place, not in your mind alone, but in a social space and a shared world.

Chapter 8

Deciding and Acting

Many of the paradoxes in this book depend on theory, or fiction, or curious mathematical facts. We are unlikely to bump into impossible objects in our daily life. But there are a multitude of paradoxes that afflict decision-making and action, some of which have spawned whole new fields of inquiry, such as game theory. Here we examine some practical puzzles that pertain to motivation, preference, knowledge, negotiation, happiness, as well as moral luck and responsibility.

Buridan's Ass

This paradox is credited to the medieval philosopher and scientist Jean Buridan (1295–1356) but it is more likely to have been invented by one of his philosophical opponents in order to lampoon his ideas.

Determinism and Fatalism

A couple of definitions are required before examining the paradox itself:

- Determinism is the philosophical doctrine that every event is determined by an unbroken chain of prior causes.
- Fatalism is the view that, since all events are determined, humans have no influence over the future.

Buridan's Ass

A hungry donkey is situated midway between two equal-sized, equally appetizing bales of hay. The creature has no reason to prefer one to the other, and so cannot choose between them. Therefore he starves to death.

At first, this does not appear to be paradoxical at all: merely a whimsical story that illustrates the difficulty involved in choosing between equally attractive options. But the paradox becomes more apparent when we consider the donkey's plight in the context of Buridan's views on free will.

Buridan advocated a form of moral determinism whereby humans, when faced with competing choices, must always choose the greater good. He held that the will cannot act independently of the intellect. Instead, it must incline toward whichever alternative the intellect judges to be most desirable.

This means that if the intellect judges two alternatives to be equally desirable, there is no way to choose between them. There is no independent faculty of will with the power to choose spontaneously, or randomly.

The paradox of the hungry donkey can therefore be seen as a reductio ad absurdum argument against Buridan's doctrine of intellect and will. Buridan's view implies that we, like the donkey, would starve to death if placed in similar circumstances. But this seems absurd, because we know that we would, in fact, make a choice.

A Challenge to Fatalism

Imagine you are hungry, and are situated midway between equally appetizing plates of food. If all of your choices and actions are causally determined, and there is nothing in your causal history to make you incline to one plate of food rather than the other, then how could you make a choice? Fatalism seems to imply that you couldn't.

And yet, surely you would. Wouldn't you?

BURIDAN'S BRIDGE

The paradox of Buridan's Ass may not have been devised by Buridan himself, but this one definitely was.

Socrates wishes to cross a river using a bridge. Plato, the bridge keeper, says, "If your next utterance is true, I will let you cross. But if it is false, I will throw you into the water." After a few moments' thought, Socrates mischievously replies, "You will throw me into the water."

Can Plato fulfill his promise?

SOLUTION

No, he cannot. If he throws Socrates into the water then Socrates spoke truly, and should have been allowed to cross. If he allows Socrates to cross, then Socrates spoke falsely, and therefore should have been thrown into the water.

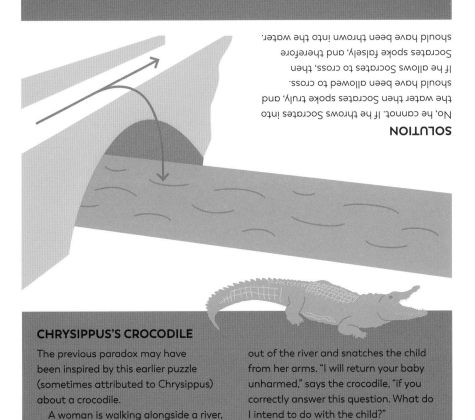

CHRYSIPPUS'S CROCODILE

The previous paradox may have been inspired by this earlier puzzle (sometimes attributed to Chrysippus) about a crocodile.

A woman is walking alongside a river, carrying her baby. A crocodile rises up out of the river and snatches the child from her arms. "I will return your baby unharmed," says the crocodile, "if you correctly answer this question. What do I intend to do with the child?"

What is the woman's best reply?

SOLUTION

She must answer, "You intend to keep it." Then, if he does intend to keep it, he must return it.

Knowledge and Free Will

In his essay on "The Art of Rational Conjecture," Bertrand Russell gives a wickedly sarcastic summary of the biblical account of The Fall: "God told [Adam and Eve] not to eat of the fruit of a certain tree, and when they nevertheless did so, He was very angry, although He had always known that they would disobey Him." Russell has a point. It does seem rather odd that the Almighty would set mankind a test, knowing that they would fail, and then get Himself all worked up about it.

Foreknowledge versus Free Will

But there is an even deeper problem. If God knew, infallibly, that Adam and Eve would eat the forbidden fruit, then how could they have done otherwise? To have resisted temptation would have been to invalidate God's infallible knowledge.

More generally, if God infallibly foreknows every human action, then there can be no free will. Why not? Because if God knows the future, then the future is fixed; and if the future is fixed, then no one has any control over it; and if no one has any control, free will is an illusion.

Conversely, if we humans do have free will, how can God foresee our future actions? He cannot predict them by deterministic laws, because then our will is not free. But how else can he predict them? How can anyone—even God— predict genuinely spontaneous choices?

It seems that either God knows the future and there is no free will; or that there is free will and God does not know the future. Those who wish to maintain both that God knows the future and that humans have free will face a dilemma. They must abandon one of their cherished beliefs—or find a way to resolve the paradox.

St. Augustine versus Cicero

The Christian bishop and philosopher, St. Augustine of Hippo (354–430 CE), wrestles with this problem in Book V of *The City of God*. To him, it was perfectly clear where Christian men and women ought to stand on the issue of foreknowledge and free will: "The religious mind chooses both, confesses both, and maintains both by the faith of piety." He was, of course, aware of the difficulties involved in maintaining both doctrines. They had been clearly enunciated by the Roman statesman and philosopher Cicero (106–43 BCE).

Cicero's argument goes like this. If all future things are foreknown by God, then there is a certain order of things which God foreknows. And if there is a certain order of things, then there must be a certain order of causes according to which those things happen. But if everything happens according to a certain order of causes, then everything happens inevitably. Therefore, "There is nothing in our power, and there is no such thing as freedom of will."

Augustine's response is very interesting. He accepts that there is a certain order of causes that leads inevitably to a predictable

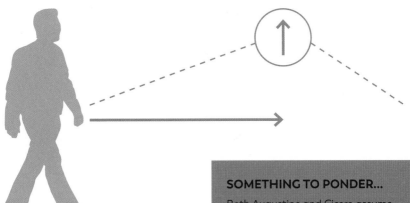

future. But he denies that this threatens the freedom of the human will, since "Our wills themselves are included in that order of causes."

What he means is this. Whenever you make a choice, that choice is determined by two factors: external circumstances and the internal workings of your will. But God has perfect knowledge of both, and is thus able to infallibly predict your actions.

This does not rule out your freedom to act, since you are exercising your will. It is just that God knows, in advance, precisely how you will exercise it.

Augustine's view, then, is that divine foreknowledge and human free will are perfectly compatible. One does not rule out the other.

SOMETHING TO PONDER...

Both Augustine and Cicero assume that divine foreknowledge requires God to predict future actions and events. But some people argue that God does not need to predict the future, He simply perceives it. How so? Because He exists outside of time. Past, present, and the future are all one to Him, and all fall under His gaze.

· Is this alternative account of God's foreknowledge any easier to reconcile with human freedom?
· Read about the block universe on pp. 138–139 to see how modern science supports the notion that past, present, and future are all equally real. Does this help make sense of the idea that God perceives the future without having to predict it?

The Predictor

This beautiful, intriguing, and frustrating puzzle was invented in 1960 by William A. Newcomb, an American physicist. It was later popularized by the philosopher Robert Nozick, and usually goes by the name Newcomb's Paradox.

One Box or Two?

You are presented with two boxes: A and B. You can't see what's inside, but you are reliably informed that box A contains $1,000, and that box B contains either $1,000,000 or nothing.

You are given a choice. You can open both of the boxes and keep the contents; or you can open just box B and keep the contents. As it stands, the decision is a no-brainer. But just before you reach out to open both boxes you are given some additional information.

The Predictor

The boxes were filled a short time ago by an entity known as the Predictor.

It doesn't really matter what kind of entity the Predictor is. You can think of it as a god, a powerful brain-scanning computer, a talented psychic, or anything you like. The important thing is that he, she, or it is able to make highly accurate predictions (amounting to near certainty) about your decisions.

When the Predictor filled the boxes, it did so according to the following rules: if it predicted that you would open only box B, it placed $1,000,000 inside it; but if it predicted that you would open both boxes, it left box B empty. In either case, it placed $1,000 inside box A.

Will you open both boxes, or just box B? Make your decision before reading on.

One Box or Two

When Robert Nozick put this problem to his friends, colleagues, and students, he discovered that the correct course of action was perfectly obvious to almost everyone. The difficulty was, in Nozick's words, "that these people seem to divide almost evenly on the problem, with large numbers thinking that the opposing side is just being silly."

It seems, then, that the world contains two very different kinds of people: "one-boxers" and "two-boxers." Let's examine the case put forward by each opposing camp.

The case for opening just one box is as follows: If you open both boxes, the Predictor will almost certainly have anticipated your choice and left box B empty. So you will get just $1,000. But if you open just box B, the Predictor will almost certainly have anticipated your choice and placed $1,000,000 in it. Clearly, therefore you should open just B.

However, the case for opening both boxes is equally clear: The Predictor has already filled both boxes. Nothing you now do can make any difference to their contents. There are, then, only two possible states of affairs: either the

Predictor has placed $1,000,000 in box B, or it hasn't.

If it has filled box B, then you ought to open both boxes. This nets you $1,000 from box A in addition to the $1,000,000 you get from box B. If the Predictor hasn't filled box B, then you still ought to open both, as $1,000 is a lot better than nothing. Either way, you ought to open both boxes.

The Paradox

Thus we have a paradox. Clear and simple reasoning demonstrates that you ought to open just box B. But equally clear and simple reasoning demonstrates that you ought to open both boxes.

There is no easy solution to Newcomb's Paradox. Indeed, there is no generally accepted solution, easy or otherwise. It is not enough, of course, for one-boxers or two-boxers merely to point to the validity of their own reasoning. They must also identity the flaw in their opponents' argument. And that is no easy matter.

A CHALLENGE

If you are a one-boxer, try to identify the flaw in the two-boxers' argument. If you are a two-boxer, try to identify the flaw in the one-boxers' argument.

Now try this...

Newcomb's problem is one of the few philosophical problems that will engage the interest of your non-philosophically minded friends. Bring it up for discussion next time you meet at the bar. See which friends are one-boxers, and which are two-boxers.

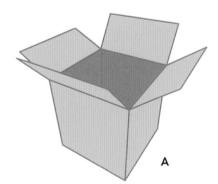

A

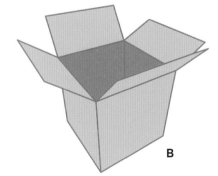

B

The Prisoner's Dilemma: Part 1

The Prisoner's Dilemma is a classic conundrum from game theory: a branch of mathematics concerned with maximizing benefits in situations where the success of an individual's choices depends upon the choices made by others.

The Dilemma

Imagine that you and I have been arrested for committing a crime and are being interrogated in separate cells. The authorities tell us that the amount of jail-time we serve will depend upon whether or not we each confess to our crime. They outline four alternatives:

- If you confess but I don't, you will go free while I serve a five-year prison sentence.
- If I confess but you don't, I will go free while you serve a five-year prison sentence.
- If we both confess, we will each serve a two-year sentence.
- If neither of us confesses, our crime cannot be proved. In that case, we will both be jailed for six months on a lesser charge.

We must each choose without knowing the other person's decision.

Now, assuming that you are indifferent to my fate, and simply want to minimize your own sentence, how should you act? Decide before reading on.

The Rational Choice

The rational choice is to confess. Why? Because, for you, confessing is the best option whatever I do.

If I confess, then your confession secures you a two-year sentence instead of the five-year one you'd get if you didn't confess. If I don't confess then your confession secures you instant freedom. Either way, you ought to confess.

But wait a moment: confessing may be the rational choice, but it has a very serious drawback. Can you work out what it is?

The drawback is that what is rational for you is rational for me. This means that I too will confess. So we will both receive a two-year prison sentence. Had we cooperated, by not confessing, we would each have received a six-month sentence. This is a much better outcome for both of us.

The paradox, then, is that the most rational choice leads us both, quite predictably, to a suboptimal outcome. But doesn't this make the "rational" choice irrational? We can both see that the decision to confess will land us with a two-year sentence. So wouldn't it be more rational to keep silent?

Sadly not. Because if I believe that you will follow this subtle line of reasoning and remain silent, the best thing that I can do is to confess. This secures my immediate freedom.

There's no getting around it. The rational thing to do is to confess: even though this leaves us both worse off than we might have been.

The Real World

The lesson to be learned from the Prisoner's Dilemma is that when individuals make rational choices based purely on self-interest they can end up worse-off than if they had cooperated.

This lesson has many applications in the real world. The Australian philosopher Peter Singer gives an example involving rush-hour traffic in his book, *How Are We to Live?*

City commuters are well aware of the problems caused by overcrowding on the roads. Now, if you are a commuter, it may well be in your best interests to drive to work. This will be quicker than taking the bus, since buses don't carry you door-to-door and also have to cope with rush-hour traffic just as cars do.

On the other hand, it would surely be better all round if everyone made a collective decision to take the bus. Bus services could then operate more frequently (because more passengers would justify operating more buses) and the buses would travel nice and quickly on the less crowded roads.

The rational, self-interested choice makes everyone worse off than they would have been had they cooperated.

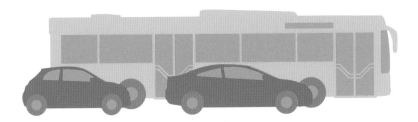

REAL-LIFE EXAMPLES

In the above example, if everyone else did make a collective decision to take the bus, wouldn't it be in your best interests to continue driving? That way you'd still have all the convenience of quieter roads, and there'd be no waiting at bus stops.

Try thinking of other real-life situations into which the Prisoner's Dilemma might offer an insight. For example, fishing quotas, reducing one's carbon footprint, and so on.

The Prisoner's Dilemma: Part 2

There's something rather grim and depressing about the Prisoner's Dilemma explained on the previous pages. It illustrates only too vividly how rational self-interested choices can make everyone worse off.

Consider, for example, two hostile nations engaged in an arms race: each committed to crippling levels of defense spending. The benefits of cooperation and the mutual reduction of arms expenditure are obvious. But it is equally obvious that unilateral defense cuts will leave one nation at the mercy of the other. Thus, rational self-interest perpetuates the arms race, and everyone loses out.

Is there nothing good that can be said for rational self-interest? Does it inevitably lead to non-cooperation and lose–lose situations?

Thankfully not. In certain situations, rational self-interest can lead to cooperation and make everyone better off. It may even offer a solution to the Prisoner's Dilemma.

The Iterated Prisoner's Dilemma

If the Prisoner's Dilemma were played out as a game, in which the player with the shortest prison sentence wins, the only sensible strategy would be to confess. This is always the best option whatever your opponent does. You would never lose by adopting this strategy.

But what if the game required the two players to reenact the Prisoner's Dilemma repeatedly, and total up their respective jail times? Or, even better, what if there were a round-robin tournament consisting of many such games, where the lowest overall score wins?

This would make a much more interesting game. Rather than always confessing, you could try adopting some more subtle and sophisticated strategies. After all, in terms of your overall tournament score, it might be worthwhile to sometimes cooperate with your opponents (by not confessing).

In fact it is possible to try out various strategies online—just search for "Iterated Prisoner's Dilemma simulation." Depending on the engine you find, you will be able to select a number of strategies, or even create your own. Give it a try; see how it works out.

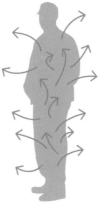

Tit-for-Tat

In 1979, social theorist Robert Axelrod organized just such a tournament. He invited experts in decision-making and game theory to submit strategies that could be fed into a computer, and left to slug it out (or cooperate nicely) with one another.

Fourteen strategies were submitted. Some were very simple; others exceedingly complex. Some were "nice" strategies based mostly on cooperation; others were "mean" strategies, biased toward confessing.

The clear winner turned out to be the simplest strategy of all. It was called "Tit-for-Tat," and consisted of just two rules:

- On the first encounter with another player, always cooperate.
- On subsequent encounters with the same player, copy whatever they did last.

Tit-for-Tat is a "nice" strategy: it begins by cooperating, and will continue to do so if given any inducement. But Tit-for-Tat is no doormat: when provoked, it will retaliate. Importantly, though, it is always ready to forgive, and will resume cooperation if another player's actions merit it.

Perhaps, then, the lesson we learn from the Prisoner's Dilemma is not so depressing after all. True, a single game requires us to adopt a self-interested strategy that makes everyone lose out. But the iterated Prisoner's Dilemma demonstrates that the rational, self-interested choice can be to cooperate—at least, with those who deserve it.

You Scratch My Back...

It is easy to see how the Tit-for-Tat strategy might be usefully applied to real-world situations. Many decisions about cooperation are not one-off matters, but crop up repeatedly. In such cases, it is often to our benefit to cooperate with others. But, crucially, only if they are willing to cooperate in turn.

For example, imagine that your car has broken down and you need help pushing it to a nearby garage. Aside from any philanthropic tendencies I may have, it is probably worth my while giving you a hand. After all, there will probably come a time when I need your help.

When that time comes, if you help me, we will find ourselves locked into a virtuous cycle of mutual cooperation. But if you refuse to help me... Well, don't ask for any more favors, that's all!

The old-fashioned practice of barn-raising, where a community comes together to assemble a barn for one of its households, provides a fine example of the self-interested benefits of cooperation on a larger scale.

Something to Ponder

Jesus said, "If someone strikes you on the right cheek, turn to him the other also. ... Give to the one who asks you, and do not turn away from the one who wants to borrow from you." (Matt. 5:38–42)

In the Iterated Prisoner's Dilemma, this would equate to an "always cooperate" strategy, which has proved far less effective than Tit-for-Tat.

But what about real life? Can turning the other cheek be a useful and sustainable strategy for dealing with others?

Profile

Epicurus

Epicurus (342–270 BCE) was born on the Aegean island of Samos, but spent most of his life in or near Athens. At that time, Athens was a depressing place. The once-glorious democracy had begun to slide into despotism and civil unrest, and many Athenians simply gave in to skepticism and despair. But not Epicurus. He devoted himself single-mindedly to finding a way of life in which happiness could flourish despite the gloomy circumstances.

Pursuing Pleasure

According to Epicurus, the aim of life is to achieve happiness by pursuing pleasure and avoiding pain (an ethical viewpoint known as hedonism: see pp. 186–187).

At first sight, this looks like a recipe for overindulgence; and that is precisely how many of Epicurus's contemporaries chose to interpret it. They accused him and his followers of leading lives of gluttony, drunkenness, and sexual depravity.

But their accusations could hardly have been more unjust. Epicurus certainly did endorse the pursuit of pleasure. But he recognized that some pleasures lead to pain and ought therefore to be avoided.

Overeating may be pleasant in the short term, but it leads to stomachaches and ill-health. A bout of drinking may be fun, but the resulting hangover is not. Wealth and power are all very well, but are not worth the stress

and anxiety that inevitably accompany them.

The pleasures Epicurus recommended were simple and lasting ones: wholesome food, the company of friends, and a simple, stress-free lifestyle. Overindulgence was definitely not on the agenda.

"I spit on luxurious pleasures," wrote Epicurus, "not for their own sake but because of the inconveniences that follow them."

This philosophy was so persuasive that Epicurus soon attracted a group of disciples, keen to put his ideas in to practice. They formed a self-sufficient community, just outside the city, and lived simply and happily together. Outsiders referred to them as the "garden philosophers."

Avoiding Pain and Fear

According to Epicurus, the avoidance of pain is every bit as important as the pursuit of pleasure. This applies as much to mental as to physical pain. We cannot achieve our goal of a happy life if we are plagued by worry, fear, stress, and anxiety.

Epicurus held that two of the greatest sources of human misery are the fear of the gods and the fear of death. But in both cases he believed that our fears are unfounded.

Epicurus believed we need not fear the gods, because although they exist they do not interfere with human affairs. Thus we cannot incur their wrath.

Furthermore, he thought that we need not fear death, because death entails the annihilation of both body and soul. There is neither sensation nor consciousness beyond the grave, and therefore no possibility of pain: "Death, the most dreaded of evils, is therefore of no concern to us; for while we exist, death is not present, and when death is present, we no longer exist."

Not everyone finds this argument consoling, but it certainly worked for Epicurus. He suffered ill-health all of his life, which eventually led to an unpleasant death. But on the very day he died, he wrote to a friend: "On this truly happy day of my life, as I am at the point of death, I write this to you. The diseases in my bladder and stomach are pursuing their usual course… but against all this is the joy in my heart at the recollection of my conversations with you."

The Epicurean Paradox

Epicurus is usually credited with being the first philosopher to discuss the problem of evil (the difficulty of reconciling the existence of evil or suffering in the world with the existence of a benevolent God). Hence, the problem of evil is sometimes referred to as the Epicurean Paradox.

In his book, *Dialogues Concerning Natural Religion*, the Scottish philosopher David Hume (1711–1776), beautifully and concisely expresses the Epicurean Paradox:

"Is [God] willing to prevent evil, but not able? Then He is impotent. Is He able, but not willing? Then He is malevolent. Is He both able and willing? Whence then is evil?"

The Paradox of Hedonism

As discussed on the previous pages, the Greek philosopher Epicurus held that happiness is the ultimate goal of life, and that the way to achieve it is to pursue pleasure and avoid pain. This ethical viewpoint is known as hedonism.

Pursuing Happiness

In practice, happiness is not so easy to acquire. Often, it seems that the tighter you try to grasp it, the more easily it slips through your fingers. As the writer C. P. Snow observed, "The pursuit of happiness is a ridiculous phrase, if you pursue happiness you'll never find it."

I can bear this out from my own experience. Some years ago, my wife Wendy and I took a career-break and went traveling. We left our home in England and spent twelve months touring the USA, New Zealand, Australia, Singapore, and Malaysia. It was a hedonist's dream—an entire year devoted to leisure, pleasure, and culture.

But something unexpected happened. During the early part of our travels, I found myself constantly fretting about how happy I was. I would look out across the Grand Canyon and think to myself: "This is one of the world's great wonders; am I enjoying it enough?"

The same thing happened at Uluru (Ayers Rock) in Australia, and at the thermal springs in New Zealand. At Niagara Falls I fretted so much the day was almost ruined.

Eventually, I made a decision to stop analyzing my feelings. It took a lot of willpower, but gradually I learned to direct my attention outward rather than inward.

By the time I reached the Great Barrier Reef I had mastered the art. I spent the day focused on the coral, the sharks, and the fish rather than myself, and had a wonderful time.

John Stuart Mill on Happiness

What I learned from this experience is neatly summed up by the English philosopher, John Stuart Mill (1806–1873): "Ask yourself whether you are happy, and you cease to be so."

This comment is all the more interesting coming from Mill, since he was the godson and erstwhile disciple of the philosopher Jeremy Bentham (1748–1832). Bentham was a hedonist par excellence. Like Epicurus, he equated happiness with pleasure, and believed that a happy life is simply one in which pleasure outweighs pain.

He even went so far as to invent a felicific calculus—a method of calculating the amount of pleasure and pain that a certain action is likely to cause. This approach has a very strong appeal. It makes the pursuit of happiness seem rational, logical, and (provided we do our calculations carefully) achievable.

So, on the face of it, few people had greater prospects for happiness than John Stuart Mill. He was intelligent and well educated, and had been brought up to know, understand, and apply Bentham's principles. But, at age 20, Mill went through a period of depression that lasted for six months.

During that time, the hyper-rational, pursue-pleasure/avoid-pain approach to happiness that he had learned from Jeremy Bentham was unable to pull him out of his misery. In fact, it was poetry—the poetry of William Wordsworth—that finally got through to him and provided the much needed "medicine for [his] state of mind."

This experience caused Mill to reassess his view on happiness. One of the insights he gained was this: "Those only are happy… who have their minds fixed on some object other than their own happiness: on the happiness of others, on the improvement of mankind, even on some art or pursuit… Aiming thus at something else, they find happiness by the way." This insight, that you can only achieve happiness by seeking something else, is often labeled the Paradox of Hedonism, or the Happiness Paradox.

SOMETHING TO THINK ABOUT

Make a list of things you do that bring you happiness; for example, participating in a favorite sport, pursuing a hobby or pastime, spending time with your children, socializing with friends, and so on.

Now, ask yourself the following question: Do you do those things because they make you happy, or are you happy because you do those things?

The Mere Addition Paradox

Faced with climate change and overpopulation, you'd think there'd be neither difficulty nor incentive for philosophers to provide ethical arguments in support of addressing these problems. However, counterintuitively, as philosopher Derek Parfit argues, there's actually a strong argument that justifies doing nothing. This is called "the Mere Addition Paradox," also known as "the repugnant conclusion."

The paradox arises from a conflict between seemingly reasonable assumptions. Most people would probably agree it's better to have a few very happy people than a much larger group of unhappy people. Adapting Parfit's example slightly, imagine that you and some friends decide to set up the ideal community on some remote island. It has everything you need—fresh water, food, resources for building and making things—and after a few years you've built yourself a paradise where everyone is extremely content. Now, let's say another group of people arrives—you don't own the island—and this doubles your population. Being new, they don't yet have the material comforts you've evolved, but

they're still pretty happy to have found this paradise, which is much better than where they were. Also, for the moment, since they've set up camp on the other side of the island, their presence doesn't affect you. Now, is the situation better or worse than before? Objectively, it's difficult to say it's worse, because your happiness hasn't been affected, and the new arrivals are better off and still pretty happy—so what's a few more people?

Diminishing Resources

However, over time the impact of the arrivals does start to affect the happiness of the original inhabitants. Resources decrease, there's less space, etc. This makes the original group very slightly less happy, but because the new arrivals are gradually establishing themselves, achieving greater comfort, their happiness has increased greatly, to a point where it's equal to what yours is now. So now, both the total *and* average happiness is higher than when the new people first arrived. Better? Objectively speaking, most would say so.

And so if this third stage of your little society is better than the previous one, and the previous was better (or at least, not worse) than the first one, then the laws of logic dictate that the third is better than the first. In other words, it's better to have a larger group of moderately happy people than a few really happy people. This doesn't seem like such a problem for your initial assumption, but Parfit hasn't finished yet . . .

Let's take your new, only slightly less happy society, into which the new arrivals have now integrated, and add some fresh paradise seekers. Problem? Not if we follow previous logic—what's a few more people, remember? But the same thing happens: the new people eventually integrate, there's less space, etc., and everyone eventually becomes marginally less happy—but with greater total and average happiness than when the second wave of new people first arrived. And then,

we repeat the process ... in fact, as long as the added lives are still worth living, adding more people always seems justified.

Diminishing Happiness

The repugnant (and seemingly paradoxical) conclusion is therefore that utilitarianism would seem to favor an overpopulated "paradise" of relatively miserable people over one of far fewer much happier people, right up to the point where it all goes *Lord of the Flies*. How did this happen? You may recognize here the tricky hand of transitivity: if B is better than A, and C is better than B, then C is better than A. Perhaps then the problem lies in one of these steps. Or is something wrong with utilitarianism itself?

FUTURE PEOPLE

Underlying Parfit's paradox is the troubling question of our obligation to future people—that is, people who don't yet exist. Perhaps you think it obvious that we should care about future generations—but why?

An action is immoral if it harms someone or impinges on their rights. But how can I harm someone who doesn't yet exist? These are, at best, hypothetical persons, and even if we could make a case for taking their interests into account, it seems dubious

that such interests should outweigh those of the currently living.

And here's the root of the problem: if we always favor the interests of those currently alive, then this would also seem to justify actions that may harm the interests of future generations. Put simply: if reversing global warming and climate change requires hardship, why would we endure that for people who don't yet exist? Utilitarianism may not have an answer to that.

Moral Robots: Part 1—Deontology

Ethical paradoxes can take different forms, depending on the theory involved. Interestingly, the latest developments in driverless cars have given fresh relevance to these debates, as questions arise as to what form of ethics should inform the behavior of the artificial intelligence that controls the vehicle.

Unsurprisingly, this type of dilemma has been well covered in science fiction, specifically in Isaac Asimov's *Robot* series. Famously, Asimov outlined three laws that were intended to ensure a robot behaved ethically (he later added a fourth, overriding law, but it's not really relevant to this discussion). Here they are, as they first appeared in his short story "Runaround":

1. A robot may not injure a human being or, through inaction, allow a human being to come to harm.
2. A robot must obey the orders given it by human beings except where such orders would conflict with the First Law.
3. A robot must protect its own existence as long as such protection does not conflict with the First or Second Laws.

Best Laid Plans

Now, these seem fairly sensible. However, as the short story itself reveals (as do, in different ways, many of the other stories in this series), the best-laid plans of men and robots sometimes go awry. In "Runaround," the robot is sent to collect a vitally needed chemical element, but hours later has still not returned. What's happened is that, unknown to its human operators, the chemical is hazardous to the robot's functioning, and so (in obedience of law 3), it refrains from approaching the chemical. However, it must also obey human commands (law 2), and since it hasn't been told that the mission is a matter of life and death (without the chemical, the humans will die), then there is nothing to override law 3. And so, it gets stuck in a paradoxical loop.

ROGUE AI

The idea that there may come a day where computers become so powerful that they try to destroy humanity is a staple of science-fiction, from HAL in *2001: A Space Odyssey*, to Skynet in the *Terminator* films, to the sentient machines of *The Matrix*. In fact, such a fear of our own rebellious creations goes back to Mary Shelley's *Frankenstein*, and beyond, to medieval stories of the golem.

But despite what certain AI enthusiasts predict, it's extremely unlikely that computers will develop any sort of autonomy, let alone "consciousness." What is more likely is that we surrender control to certain systems and automated protocols, which—as with any unconscious processes—are likely at some point to go wrong in unforeseen ways.

Of course, it may be argued, even such imperfect systems may be preferable: there will likely be far fewer accidents with driverless cars than with human operated ones.

Rule-Based Ethics

We can easily see ways around this, of course, and it would be easy to program a simple solution. However, the example raises a fundamental question for rule-based ethics: what happens when there is a conflict between rules? Rule-based morality is sometimes referred to as *deontology*, which is basically the contention that fundamental to morality is the notion of duty. You behave ethically because you have a duty to do so. This emphasis is central to the philosophy of Kant, who argued that our ultimate duty is to reason, which—happily—dictates what is moral. And so, as long as we follow the dictates of reason, we should be fine. So, what does reason dictate? Kant formulated this in various ways, but the basic thrust is that moral choices must be universalizable. That is, we should act in such a way that we would be happy for anyone else to do the same. This rules out lying and stealing and murder and all those things that we wouldn't want to be on the receiving end of, and seems in general to give a good account of morality.

But how would a Kantian robot fare? A famous objection to Kant arises in relation to conflicting duties: if it is wrong to lie, and it is also wrong to harm another human being, what happens if telling the truth results in someone else's harm? As with the robot, the conflict would seem to result in a paradox. Furthermore, in relation to our driverless car, following some absolute rule such as "not to injure a human being or allow it to come to harm" would not seem to help when the only choice is between (e.g.) one pedestrian or five. As such, perhaps a deontological robot isn't such a good idea. But what is the alternative?

Moral Robots: Part 2—Consequentialism

Returning to the driverless car dilemma: even if it's been pre-programmed to save human life, there'll be situations where injury or death are unavoidable. Curiously, in relation to current driving practices, the moral imperatives are not always spelled out: for instance, the UK highway code states that, if it cannot be safely avoided, a driver may run over small animals. But nowhere does it also say, "Also try to avoid killing people if you can"—it is simply presumed that you will do so. And maybe that's the problem: many of the split-second decisions we may be faced with as motorists rely on moral intuitions that we may not be fully conscious of.

This is brought out by *The Trolley Problem*, a famous thought experiment first proposed by the philosopher Philippa Foot, but later responded to and enlarged upon by subsequent philosophers. Imagine that there is a runaway trolley (or train), and that it is headed for a group of five people working on the track. On another track there is a single person. Your only option is to switch tracks (or not), and whoever is on the chosen track will certainly be killed. Approached from a deontological approach, there would seem to be no clear answer: both options contravene the rule not to harm. Furthermore, by flicking the switch you become morally responsible for that harm. It's lose-lose.

Preferable Outcomes

But the correct response in real-life situations often isn't easy or clear, and a decision has to be made one way or another. For this reason, a better option is a consequentialist approach. Let's forget about absolute rules, for the moment, and ask ourselves, of the two, which is the preferable outcome. And the answer seems

simple, doesn't it? Utilitarianism, which is a form of consequentialism, would look at the dilemma and say that five lives outweigh one, and that we actually have a moral responsibility to switch. So, do you? But what if you were told that the five individuals were serial killers on a work-release program from prison? Or that the individual was a well-known philanthropist, or even a member of your family? Would that alter your decision?

Morality Is More Than Statistics

Returning to Asimov—or, rather, the film loosely based on his stories, *I, Robot*—we are presented with a similarly utilitarian calculation. Will Smith's car plunges off a bridge into a river, along with another car, containing a young girl; a robot dives in to rescue them, but realizes that he cannot save both, and Smith has the best chances of survival. In the film, the robot's decision explains Smith's animosity to robots: most people would have rescued the child first, no matter what their survival chances. Morality, the scenario implies, is not a matter of cold statistical calculation, but involves a subjective and emotional element. Problematically, this also means that people will likely disagree on the morally right thing to do for ultimately personal reasons—even philosophers.

Of course, whatever system we program into the AI, it's unlikely that it will result in moral decisions that will always make everyone happy. Even if it were some sort of Laplace's Demon, the potential factors and consequences that would need to be weighed would theoretically stretch

on forever—yes, the single individual is a philanthropist, but he is also destined to invest in some bio-tech company that will shortly inadvertently release some terrible plague, or whatever. All this might not be strictly paradoxical, but it does seem to suggest that any ethical system, whether deontological or consequentialist, is incapable of always determining the "right" action—even according to its own rules and principles.

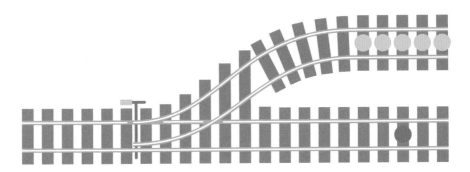

THE PAPERCLIP MAXIMIZER

The problem with consequentialism is that it can occasionally seem to justify courses of action that are (by traditional standards) morally wrong, or even abhorrent. If the suffering of an innocent would benefit the greatest number, then that course of action would be justified.

This is the sort of thing that a deontological robot could rule out (we simply build in the rule that "innocents must not be harmed")—though of course, as we've seen, this would not help in situations where such harm was

unavoidable. However, if the means justify the ends, then arguably, a consequentialist robot is more likely to go wrong.

Imagine (says philosopher Nick Bostrom) an intelligent machine tasked with producing paperclips. Since this is its primary goal, it will utilize all means to maximize its paperclip output—even, eventually, to the point where human beings, the planet, the universe itself, merely provide raw materials for paperclip manufacture.

Exercise 8

Deciding and Acting

THE PROBLEM:

Intolerance is intolerable. It follows that we must not tolerate intolerance. It follows, too, that we must tolerate intolerance, for it would be intolerable for us to stoop to intolerance. We must not tolerate what is intolerable, but we must also tolerate it, lest we lower ourselves to the level of the intolerant, and commit the same intolerable wrong as they do. Prove that the foregoing is moral nonsense by exploding the paradoxes within it.

THE METHOD:

To tolerate something, if we are to speak precisely, is to object to it, yet to find it within some threshold, and so nevertheless to accept it. Toleration consists in three moments: an objection, an acceptance, and an implied limit of acceptance, or threshold of rejection. Each aspect is necessary, and each is home to paradox.

To tolerate something is to accept it, but unless one also objects to it, one is not tolerating it at all but simply accepting it, with indifference perhaps or even approval. We must regard something as wrong if we are properly said to be tolerating it. So in tolerating something, we accept what we regard as wrong. If we think it right to tolerate it (it falls within a certain threshold, beyond which lies

intolerable wrongs) then we think it wrong not to tolerate this wrong. But how can it be morally right to tolerate what is morally wrong? This is the acceptance paradox.

Now consider certain racists, who think their own race is superior to others, and would suppress all those they consider inferior, if they could. However, whether out of impotence or fear of reprisal or expectation of arrest and imprisonment, these racists manage to restrain themselves. We say they now tolerate others, and we encourage them in this toleration. But should we praise them for the virtue of tolerance, when it is really hate hemmed in by prudence? Their tolerance is apparently all the greater, the more they regard themselves as superior and others suitable for oppression. Paradoxically, this seems to strengthen a virtue by an increase of vice. Extremely hateful yet restrained racists would then be paragons of virtue.

A third paradox concerning toleration arises from the necessity to draw a limit, to impose a threshold, beyond which lies the intolerable. Without such a limit, toleration is no virtue, but at best an untested laxity. And yet to set a threshold is to be intolerant of all that passes beyond that threshold. So the act of toleration requires intolerance in principle. Toleration as a virtue defeats itself, and obliterates itself as soon as it exists.

THE SOLUTION:

Each of these paradoxes is more illusion than genuine paradox, and arises from inadvertent confusion of distinct meanings of "tolerance."

The acceptance paradox is resolved by distinguishing moral reasons of different orders. Acceptance and rejection come with variable costs, and what is tolerable is a matter of degree, so that a situation can be more or less intolerable. It may not be worth the trouble to close down what, if intensified, might need ending at any cost. Some principles may be inviolable, others defeasible, violations of which, for both practical and principled reasons, it might sometimes be wise to accept. So there is no inherent problem in accepting what one objects to, as long as one is not accepting or objecting to it for the same reason (but for a higher reason).

The tolerant racists paradox trades on the objection inherent to toleration: one must object to what one tolerates. Indeed, the more they objected, the more virtuous they appeared (when, for whatever practical or strategic reasons, they were able to restrain themselves). This self-restraint now takes on the paradoxical aspect of

tolerance by the intolerant, a virtue of the vicious. And yet it is not, after all, an ethical virtue. In the circumstance, it may be called an ethical duty, and as such is properly to be expected, rather than worthy of praise or esteem, as virtues are. Even then their restraint is compliance with duty rather than duty for duty's sake, for it is at best prudential and instrumental, not ethical at all. Thus the tolerant racist is really only tolerant if tolerance is not an ethical virtue.

Moreover, virtues are never merely behaviorally defined, but have an inward component, which in the case of tolerance is satisfied by respect but not by hatred. It may be good and right to prevent the expression of one's hatred, but it is neither if it is only done to be more hateful and intolerant at some later time. And however good and right it may be, it would be better still, and unquestionably a moral excellence, to rid oneself of hatred altogether. That is how to increase the virtue of tolerance, which requires of the racist less self-restraint and more self-overcoming.

The third paradox involves the necessity and the simultaneous impossibility of drawing a limit to toleration without overstepping it. To call something tolerable is to warn that, beyond a certain point, it must be rejected. But this paradox too is resolved by distinguishing duty (principles that must not be violated) and virtue (what is the morally excellent, supererogatory, over and above the call of duty). The intolerant, in so far as they violate ethical principles, must not be tolerated, any more than we tolerate other lapses of duty. But the modality of injunction upon ourselves to tolerate the intolerant is not duty, but calls on all our strength and forbearance, all our compassion and understanding, in a word, our virtue.

Index of Philosophers

Hausdorff, Felix (mathematician)
Dates: 1868–1942
Nationality: German
Famous Work:
Remarks on Sets of Points
Related Paradox:
The Banach–Tarski Paradox
(the Pea and the Sun) on
pp. 168–169

Hawking, Stephen (physicist)
Dates: 1942–2018
Nationality: English
Famous Work:
A Brief History of Time
Related Paradoxes:
Laws governing time travel
on p. 140

Hegel, Georg
Dates: 1770–1831
Nationality: German
Famous Work:
Science of Logic
Related Paradox:
Identity on p. 70

Hempel, Carl Gustav
Dates: 1905–1997
Nationality: German-
American
Famous Work:
*Studies in Logic and
Confirmation*
Related Paradox:
Hempel's Paradox
(the Paradox of the Crows)
on pp. 30–31

Heraclitus
Dates: c.535–475 BCE
Nationality: Greek
Famous Work:
On Nature
Related Paradox:
The River of Heraclitus
on pp. 46–47

Hilbert, David
Dates: 1862–1943
Nationality: German
Famous Work:
On the Infinite
Related Paradox:
Hilbert's Hotel on pp. 94–95

Hume, David
Dates: 1711–1776
Nationality: Scottish
Famous Works:
*A Treatise of Human Nature;
Dialogues Concerning
Natural Religion*
Related Paradox:
Hume's Fork on pp. 28–29

James, William
Dates: 1842–1910
Nationality: American
Famous Work:
Principles of Psychology
Related Paradox:
The dialogical self on p. 71

Landau, Edmund (mathematician)
Dates: 1877–1938
Nationality: German
Famous Works:
*Foundations of Analysis;
Differential and Integral
Calculus; Elementary
Number Theory*
Related Paradox:
The Two-Envelope Paradox
on pp. 114–117

Locke, John
Dates: 1632–1704
Nationality: English
Famous Works:
*Essay Concerning Human
Understanding;
On Toleration*

Mill, John Stuart
Dates: 1806–1873
Nationality: English
Famous Works:
On Liberty; Utilitarianism
Related Paradox:
Happiness on pp.186–187

Moore, G. E
Dates: 1873–1958
Nationality: English
Famous Works:
*Principia Ethica;
The Refutation of Idealism*
Related Paradox:
Moore's Paradox on p. 20

Newton, Sir Isaac (physicist)
Dates: 1643–1727
Nationality: English
Famous Works:
*Philosophiæ Naturalis Principia
Mathematica; Opticks*
Related Paradoxes:
Paradoxes of time travel on
p. 135

Nozick, Robert
Dates: 1938–2002
Nationality: American
Famous Works:
*Anarchy, State, Utopia;
Philosophical Explanations*
Related Paradox:
Newcomb's Paradox on
pp. 178–179

Index

References

In most cases throughout this book direct references have been omitted in order to improve the ease of reading. The references and further reading given below are listed alphabetically under each chapter heading.

Introduction

Sainsbury, R. M. (1995) *Paradoxes* (second edition). Cambridge: Cambridge University Press.

Chapter 1: Knowing and Believing

Ayer, A. J. (2000) *Hume: A Very Short Introduction (Very Short Introductions)*. Oxford: Oxford University Press.

Clark, M. (2007) *Paradoxes from A to Z* (second edition). New York: Routledge.

Cornman, J. W., Lehrer, K., and Pappas, G. S. (1991) *Philosophical Problems and Arguments: An Introduction*. Indianapolis: Hackett Publishing.

Descartes, R. (2003) *Meditations and Other Metaphysical Writings* (tr. Clarke, D. M). London: Penguin Classics.

Fearne, N. (2002) *Zeno and the Tortoise: How to Think Like a Philosopher*. London: Atlantic Books.

Graham, R. (2006) *The Great Infidel: A Life of David Hume*. East Linton: Tuckwell Press.

Hume, D. (2004) *An Enquiry Concerning Human Understanding*. New York: Dover Publications.

Hume, D. (1990) *Dialogues Concerning Natural Religion*. London: Penguin Classics.

James, W. (2003) *The Will to Believe, and Other Essays in Popular Philosophy*. New York: Dover Publications.

Jones, G., Hayward, J, and Cardinal, D. (2005) *The Meditations: René Descartes (Philosophy in Focus)*. London: Hodder Murray.

Leiber, J. (1993) *Paradoxes*. London: Gerald Duckworth & Co. Ltd.

Magee, B. (1988) *The Great Philosophers*. Oxford: Oxford University Press.

Moeller, H. G. (2004) *Daoism Explained: From the Dream of the Butterfly to the Fishnet Allegory*. Chicago: Open Court Publishing.

Plato. (1997) *Complete Works* (ed. Hutchinson, D.S.). Indianapolis: Hackett Publishing.

Russell, B. (2004) *History of Western Philosophy* (second edition). London: Routledge Classics.

Schilpp, P. A. (ed.) (1952) *The Philosophy of G. E. Moore* (second edition). New York: Tudor Publishing.

Warburton, N. (2004) *Philosophy the Basics* (fourth edition). London: Routledge.

"Sorites Paradox" from the Stanford Internet Encyclopedia of Philosophy, online version (www.stanford.edu) 2008.

Waterfield, R. (ed.). (2000) *The First Philosophers: The Presocratics and Sophists*. Oxford: Oxford University Press.

Williamson, T. (1996) *Vagueness*. London: Routledge.

Chapter 2: Vagueness and Identity

Clark, M. (2007) *Paradoxes from A to Z* (second edition). New York: Routledge.

Cohen, M. (2007) *101 Philosophy Problems*. London: Routledge.

Fox, M. A. "A New Look at Personal Identity." *Philosophy Now*, 62, July/August 2007.

"Heraclitus" from the Stanford Internet Encyclopedia of Philosophy, online version (www.stanford.edu) 2008.

Moline, J. (1969) "Aristotle, Eubulides and the Sorites." *Mind*, 78, 393–407.

Noonan, H. W. (2003) *Personal Identity* (second edition). London: Routledge.

Plato. (1997) *Complete Works* (ed. Hutchinson, D. S.). Indianapolis: Hackett Publishing.

Read, S. (1995) *Thinking About Logic: An Introduction to the Philosophy of Logic*. Oxford: Oxford University Press.

Sorensen, R. (2003) *A Brief History of the Paradox*. Oxford: Oxford University Press.

Chapter 3: Logic and Truth

Davis, M. (ed.) (2004) *The Undecidable: Basic Papers on Undecidable Propostions, Unsolvable Problems and Computable Functions*. New York: Dover Publications.

Descartes, R. (2003) *Meditations and Other Metaphysical Writings* (tr. Clarke, D. M). London: Penguin Classics.

Gödel, K. (2003) *On Formally Undecidable Propositions of "Principia Mathematica" and Related Systems*. New York: Dover Publications.

Grattan-Guinness, I. (1998) "Structural Similarity or Structuralism? Comments on Priest's Analysis of the Paradoxes of Self-Reference." *Mind*, 107, 823–834

Hegel, G. (1998) *Science of Logic* (tr. Miller, A. V.). New York: Prometheus Books.

Hothersall, D. (2004) *History of Psychology* (fourth edition). New York: McGraw-Hill

James, W. (1957) *Principles of Psychology: Volume 1* (new edition). New York: Dover Publications.

Jeans, J. (1942). *Physics and Philosophy.* Cambridge: Cambridge University Press.

Locke, J. (1996) *An Essay Concerning Human Understanding.* Indianapolis: Hackett Publishing.

Picard, M. (2007). *This is Not a Book: Adventures in Popular Philosophy.* New York: Metro Books/London: Continuum Books/ Crows Nest: Allen & Unwin.

Quine, W. V. (1980) *From a Logical Point of View: Nine Logico-Philosophical Essays* (second edition). Cambridge, Mass.: Harvard University Press.

Quine, W. V. (1976) On a Supposed Antinomy in *The Ways of Paradox, and Other Essays.* Cambridge, Mass.: Harvard University Press.

Reach. K. (1938) The name relation and the logical antinomies. *Journal of Symbolic Logic,* 3, 97–111.

Russell, B. (1908) Mathematical Logic as Based on the Theory of Types. *American Journal of Mathematics,* 30, 3, 222–262

Russell, B. (1905) On Denoting. *Mind,* 14, 56, 479-493.

Russell, B. (1996) *The Principles of Mathematics.* New York: W. W. Norton & Co.

Sainsbury, R. M. (1988) *Paradoxes.* Cambridge: Cambridge University Press.

Shen Yuting. (1955) Two Semantical Paradoxes. *Journal of Symbolic Logic,* 20 (2), 11–120.

Smullyan, R. (1985) *To Mock a Mockingbird.* Oxford: Oxford University Press.

Sorensen, R. A. (1982). "Recalcitrant Variations of the Predication Paradox." *Australasian Journal of Philosophy,* 60, 355–62.

Chapter 4: Mathematical Paradoxes

Barrow, J. D. (2005) *The Infinite Book: A Short Guide to the Boundless, Timeless and Endless.* New York: Vintage, Random House.

Bunch, B. (1997) *Mathematical Fallacies and Paradoxes.* New York: Dover Publications.

Clark, M. (2007) *Paradoxes from A to Z* (second edition). New York: Routledge.

De Morgan, A. (2007) *A Budget of Paradoxes.* New York: Cosimo Inc.

Everdell, W. R. (1998) *The First Moderns: Profiles in the Origins of Twentieth-Century Thought.* Chicago: University of Chicago Press.

Galilei, G. (2003) *Dialogues Concerning Two New Sciences* (tr. Crew, H. and de Salvio, A.). New York: Dover Publications.

Hughes, P. and Brecht, G. (1978) *Vicious Circles and Infinity: An Anthology of Paradoxes.* London: Penguin.

Kaplan, R. and Kaplan, E. (2003) *The Art of the Infinite: Our Lost Language of Numbers.* London: Penguin.

Russell, B. (2007) *Introduction to Mathematical Philosophy*. New York: Routledge.

Weston, A. (2001) *A Rulebook for Arguments* (third edition). Indianapolis: Hackett Publishing.

Chapter 5: Probability Paradoxes

Bunch, B. (1997) *Mathematical Fallacies and Paradoxes*. New York: Dover Publications.

Clark, M. (2007) *Paradoxes from A to Z* (second edition). New York: Routledge.

Gardner, M. (1986) *Knotted Doughnuts and Other Mathematical Entertainments*. New York: W. H. Freeman and Co.

Haddon, M. (2004) *The Curious Incident of the Dog in the Night-Time*. New York: Red Fox, Random House.

Haigh, J. (1999). *Taking Chances*. Oxford: Oxford University Press.

Hammond, N. (ed.) (2003) *The Cambridge Companion to Pascal*. Cambridge: Cambridge University Press.

Leiber, J. (1993) *Paradoxes*. London: Gerald Duckworth & Co. Ltd.

Mackie, J. M. (1982) *The Miracle of Theism: Arguments for and Against the Existence of God*. Oxford: Oxford University Press.

Martin, R. (2004) The St. Petersburg Paradox, in *The Stanford Encyclopedia of Philosophy* (ed. Zalta, E. N.). Stanford: Stanford University.

Pascal, B. (1995) *Pensées* (tr. Krailsheimer, A. J.). London: Penguin.

Rumsey, D. (2006) *Probability for Dummies*. Chichester: John Wiley & Sons.

Sorensen, R. A. (2003) *A Brief History of the Paradox*. Oxford: Oxford University Press.

Stewart, I. (2003) *The Magical Maze: Seeing the World through Mathematical Eyes*. Chichester: John Wiley & Sons.

Tijms, H. (2007) *Understanding Probability: Chance Rules in Everyday Life* (second edition). Cambridge: Cambridge University Press.

vos Savant, Marilyn (1990). "Ask Marilyn," *Parade Magazine*, 16.

Warburton, N. (2004) *Philosophy the Basics* (fourth edition). London: Routledge.

Chapter 6: Space and Time

Barnes, J. (1989) *The Presocratic Philosophers*. London: Routledge

Bunch, B. (1997) *Mathematical Fallacies and Paradoxes*. New York: Dover Publications.

Calle, C. I. (2005) *Einstein for Dummies*. Chichester: John Wiley & Sons.

Davies, P. (2002) *How to Build a Time Machine*. London: Penguin.

Deutsch, D. and Lockwood, M. (1994) The Quantum Physics of Time Travel. *Scientific American*, 270, 3, 68–74.

Fearne, N. (2002) *Zeno and the Tortoise: How to Think Like a Philosopher*. London: Atlantic Books.

Gott, R. (2002) *Time Travel in Einstein's Universe*. London: Phoenix, Orion.

Hughes, P. and Brecht, G. (1978) *Vicious Circles and Infinity: An Anthology of Paradoxes*. London: Penguin.

Lewis, D. (1993) "The Paradoxes of Time Travel," in *The Philosophy of Time* (ed. le Poidevin, R. and MacBeath, M.). Oxford: Oxford University Press.

McMahon, D. (2006) *Relativity Demystified*. New York: McGraw-Hill

Russell, B. (1997) *ABC of Relativity*. London: Routledge.

Russell, B. (2004) *History of Western Philosophy* (second edition). London: Routledge Classics.

Sainsbury, R. M. (1995) *Paradoxes* (second edition). Cambridge: Cambridge University Press.

Sorensen, R. A. (2003) *A Brief History of the Paradox*. Oxford: Oxford University Press.

Waterfield, R. (ed.). (2000) *The First Philosophers: The Presocratics and Sophists*. Oxford: Oxford University Press.

Chapter 7: Impossibilities

Barrow, J. D. (1998) *Impossibility: The Limits of Science and the Science of Limits*. Oxford: Oxford University Press.

Heamekers, M. http://im-possible.info/ english/art/sculpture/hemaekers_unity. html. Website of Vlad Alexeev http://im-possible.info/russian/art/ reutersvard/reut3.html

Ehrenstein, W. (1930) "Untersuchungen über Figur-Grund-Fragen." *Zeitschrift für Psychologie*, 117, 339–412.

Freidman, D. and Cycowicz, Y. (2006) "Repetition Priming of Possible and Impossible Objects from ERP and Behavioral Perspectives." *Psychophysiology*, 43, 569–78.

Gregory, R. L. (1970) *The Intelligent Eye*. London: Wiedenfeld and Nicolson.

Shuwairi, S. M., Albert, M. K., and Johnson, S. P. (2002) "Discrimination of Possible and Impossible Objects in Infancy." *Psychological Science*, 18 (4), 303–7.

Stewart, I. (1995) "Paradox of the Spheres." *New Scientist*, Jan 14, 28–31.

Wagon, S. (1985) *The Banach–Tarski Paradox*. Cambridge: CUP.

Wapner, L. M. (2005) *The Pea and the Sun: A Mathematical Paradox.* Wellesley, Mass.: A. K. Peters.

Chapter 8: Deciding and Acting

Augustine. (1872) "The City of God, Book V," in *The Works of Aurelius Augustine* (ed. Dods. M.) Edinburgh: T. & T. Clark.

Axelrod, R. (2006) *The Evolution of Cooperation.* New York: Basic Books.

Chadwick, H. (2001) *Augustine: A Very Short Introduction (Very Short Introductions).* Oxford: Oxford University Press.

Clark, M. (2007) *Paradoxes from A to Z* (second edition). New York: Routledge.

Epicurus. (1993) *Essential Epicurus: Letters, Principal Doctrines, Vatican Sayings and Fragments* (tr. O'Connor, E. M.). New York: Prometheus Books.

"Foreknowledge and Free Will" in *Stanford Internet Encyclopedia of Philosophy*, online version (www.stanford.edu) 2008.

Gardner, M. (1986) *Knotted Doughnuts and Other Mathematical Entertainments.* New York: W. H. Freeman and Co.

Hume, D. (1990) *Dialogues Concerning Natural Religion.* London: Penguin Classics.

Klima, G. (2008) John Buridan (Great Medieval Thinkers). Oxford: Oxford University Press.

Leiber, J. (1993) *Paradoxes.* London: Gerald Duckworth & Co. Ltd.

Mill, J. S. (1944) *Autobiography of John Stuart Mill.* New York: Columbia University Press.

Nozick, R. (1969) "Newcomb's Problem and Two Principles of Choice," in *Essays in Honor of Carl G. Hempel: A Tribute on the Occasion of His Sixty-Fifth Birthday* (ed. Rescher, N.). Norwell: Kluwer Academic Publishers.

Russell, B. (1997) *The Art of Philosophizing and Other Essays.* Lanham: Littlefield, Adams.

Russell, B. (2004) *History of Western Philosophy* (second edition). London: Routledge Classics.

Sainsbury, R. M. (1995) *Paradoxes* (second edition). Cambridge: Cambridge University Press.

Singer, P. (1997) *How Are We to Live?* Oxford: Oxford University Press.

Sorensen, R. A. (2003) *A Brief History of the Paradox.* Oxford: Oxford University Press.

Credits

Gareth Southwell is a philosopher, writer and illustrator. He is the author of several philosophy books including *What Would Marx Do?* (Octopus Books), *50 Philosophy of Science Ideas You Really Need to Know* (Quercus), and *A Beginner's Guide to Nietzsche's Beyond Good and Evil* (both for Wiley-Blackwell).

He has taught and written about philosophy for students and the general reader and from 2000 until 2016 he ran the website Philosophy Online, to support fellow teachers, students and those new to philosophy.

Gary Hayden is a freelance writer based in Ho Chi Min City, Vietnam. He has degrees in Physics and Philosophy, and specializes in making scientific and philosophical concepts accessible to the general reader. Gary's articles have appeared in dozens of magazines and newspapers around the world, including *The Times Educational Supplement*, *The Scotsman, Maxim*, and Singapore's national newspaper, *The Straits Times*.

Dr. Michael Picard is an MIT trained philosopher, international author, and lecturer at the University of Victoria, Canada. Trained in mathematical logic and analytic philosophy, he has taught widely in psychology and philosophy, as well as in applied programs such as leadership and environmental and business management. He is the founding leader of Cafe Philosophy, weekly community-based philosophy dialogs in Victoria that have gone on for 12 years and surpassed 500 sessions.

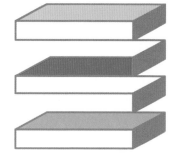